MEET MAMA BEAR

LESSONS AND STORIES FROM MY MOTHER

By Kristen Morris

DEDICATED TO:

Mama Bear's Friends

After Mom's death I found a list of names she had intended to write final notes to:

Tracy,
Gerry,
Janie,
Sandra,
Jeannie,
Pam,
Lynda,
and Scott.

I thank you each individually for the listening, learning, laughing, living, and loving you shared with her. Each of you fortified, enjoyed, taught, and blessed her. Each of you were there for her in her life in moments when no one else was. She loved you deeply, and you were on her mind in her final thoughts.

I also thank the groups throughout her life: the friends from her childhood neighborhood and local public schools, college room and classmates, fellow nurses, Army staff, cruise and travel buddies, her "older" church friends who were married with children, her peers as a single lady (the cake decorating, the Chinese food on futons, the baby-sitting, the women she came home to at the end of the day), anyone who received a wedding invitation from her, The "Eagles Mere" Ladies, the ones who hosted all her many showers, the sports moms, the women in small group, the teachers and coaches who helped train her children (especially the ones who took them under her wing during her sick and dying years), Shelley, our extended family, anyone who has spent time drawing out and reaching out to the Snyder children, the pastors' families, the strangers who left meals at the door, the friends who visited her when she moved, who sat with her during chemotherapy, and anyone who attended her memorial service or prayed, sent gifts, fed us, and acted on your care.

You were her friend, and ours too. If you are included on this list anywhere, I have probably heard your name and Mom has told me a story of some sort about you (I drilled her with questions most of my life, and nearly interviewed her about every person she knew or remembered). Your love for us through your connection to her has changed my life. I do not take your impact and effort for granted. I dedicate this book, and in very much my life, to following in your strong, generous example of being a true friend.

Thank you.

SPECIAL THANKS TO:

Becca Kless, Don Shorey, my Dad, and my Husband for using their time, talent, intellect, and skill with words to help me produce this book. I couldn't have done it without you!

TABLE OF CONTENTS

PREFACE

by Alan Snyder, Papa Bear

Many years ago, my father, a purple-heart decorated World War II veteran, had a short anecdote published in a very prominent city magazine. It went something like this:

> "A friend asked me recently if I was going to see the movie "The Battle of the Bulge?" No, I responded, I saw the play."

I saw the play, as well. From watching my 29 year old fiancée continue to pour her life into serving and baby-sitting the children of friends from our church and preparing for her own eventual motherhood, to the final days of her walk here on earth when she prepared her children for life without her, I was there in the front row watching Suzanne Snyder mother her children. Mama Bear.

There is not a more complete and informed view then the one I had the honor of watching for 26 years. Writing from that perspective would take volumes, not chapters. In this book, my daughter, writes about the effect that her mother had on her throughout the course of her life and in many specific and significant areas. I observed the process, from start to finish. Despite the impact communicated in the ensuing chapters, I can only tell you that it pales in comparison to the impact that watching (and occasionally participating) in the process had on me. I was mostly a student in a classroom.

The classroom began in the Bradley birthing classes, where we prepared for what would become the delivery of seven children. The course was being set, the priorities being defined, and the future was being framed. Her life would be one given completely to the care, nurturing and loving of her children. I dare say that few have done it with more complete commitment, more resolve, more endurance and more selflessness.

The preparation and birthing of our first child, Kristen, should have been my first insight into parenting, but it surely was my first insight into Mama Bear. A fiercely loyal, committed, caring, loving and creative role that gave me a view into the next 25 years. Watching someone lay down their life completely for someone else (seven someones to be exact, plus the two who miscarried that she is already seeing again in Heaven), it was a pre-cursor of all that was to come, some of which you are now able to share here in this book.

Most of what I learned about being a committed Christian, I learned from her. Most of what I learned about being a good father, I learned from her. Most of what I learned about bravery and commitment, I learned from her. And most of what I learned about dying gracefully, I learned from her. My hope is that, in her absence, I can successfully apply all that I have learned. She had lessons for us all.

The process of watching my children come to terms with and mourn the loss of their mother has been bitter-sweet. The excruciating pain, the demoralizing lack of understanding, the guilt associated with personal failings that diminished the quality of their relationship with her, the confusing sense of instability and lack of purpose, all weigh on me as I watch them wrestle with the truth that she is no longer there for them. This is magnified by the realization that no matter how much harder I work, I can only be more of me. I can't be her. She and she alone is their Mama Bear.

But this book and its contents point to another truth, one that rises like a phoenix from the ashes of her death. That among the greatest attributes of her mothering, she was at best a great gardener. She planted seeds for 26 years, from talking to our children in her womb, to sitting on her final bed and sharing her love. She was planting seeds the entire time, and cultivating them throughout her life. I didn't understand this at first, all the effort that went into designing the most creative birthday parties ever, to keeping journals of their childhood, to taking picture after picture after picture, to making special memories of just about everything. She had a vision. She understood. Those seeds she planted and cultivated are still coming up from the ground where she returned. They are expressions of her love, of her life, of her investment. Now that she is gone, I truly understand. She understood well before, when it really counted.

These seeds are now bringing life-giving food to the children who hunger for their Mama Bear. This book is proof. The seedlings will continue to grow around them, and they will see her more and more as time goes on. They will start planting their own seedlings as well. They will do so faithfully, diligently and lovingly because they had a model to learn from. As did I.

We all saw the play.

1. INTRODUCTION

We stood, lined up and wiggly, outside the church auditorium in red-plaid outfits, large bows, and shiny shoes. The children's choir had practiced for several nights, but now the Christmas Eve performance was upon us. This moment was nothing like the dress rehearsal or my second grade Helen Keller class play (my only other stage performance). The orchestra boomed through the doors and when it was our turn to walk the side-aisles to the stage — there were faces. Hundreds, perhaps over a thousand, faces. The night before, those faces had only been empty, purple seats. A far cry from twenty moms in the lunch room for Helen Keller.

The difference affected me immediately as I turned to walk down that aisle. My mouth suddenly was filled with sand, my eyes felt dry, my heart raced, and the cool auditorium was making me sweat. While Joseph delivered his lines loudly, all The Faces were cheerfully distracted by a line of nervous, cute children "sneaking" in from behind.

My cheeks were brushed with blush. My curls were secured with spray. I was ready, so I thought. But no amount of practice or choir-director encouragements could prepare me for this frightening moment. There were so many faces. An amused sighing "awww" floated through the auditorium. The well-worn chairs creaked under the jolly and obligated bums turning to see us. Nervous butterflies and queasiness fluttered within me — and a strange desire to cry and laugh. I was too afraid to do either.

Then, I saw her.

The whole room was a monotone picture to me, but her face was in color. My mom looked beautiful in a black velvet jacket with a shiny mistletoe pin on the lapel. She, too, had blush on her cheeks and spray in her hair. Of course, we had got ready together. She only wore make-up and sprayed her "yellow perfume" for special events. Waving and waving with one hand, she held the flashing camera with the other, smiling wide the whole time. She didn't need to wave, I saw her as if she had a spotlight on her.

Seeing her was equally relieving and embarrassing, and I sucked in my cheeks like a fish to fight off a smile. The candlelit auditorium felt much bigger than it did when we played dodgeball during recess. As we assumed our positions (mine in the center front row) I scanned the crowd again — to find her. The lights were bright as we sang our squeaky rendition of "Mary, Did You Know?" and I knew she was watching me, as if I was singing only to my mom.

***

That "face-in-a-crowd" sensation. Being looked for. The experience where all other faces blur and gray and your eyes stop on one. As we galloped around the merry-go-round in Fantasyland, she watched for us and hollered every time we passed. After school pick-up with the whole elementary school in a large lobby, she could find our heads in a herd of cloned uniforms. In those chaotic fast-food play lands, even the sound of our fun was particular to us and she knew it. Her presence was well-known on any field or at any court. In a crowded pavilion or mall or pool she could keep tabs on us — she couldn't help but keep tabs on us. While I lost track of reality in the ocean and lined my swimsuit with sand, she watched. We were her faces in every crowd, and she was ours. An invisible chain bound this little fleet of floating boats and mother-anchor.

Mom died on January 22, 2014 after fighting breast cancer for 10 years.

Just a few days later the Varsity boys' basketball team had their senior night at a home-game. Dad was the head coach and my brother Kevin was a senior starter. They walked out onto the court, accepted a rose, and — for the first time ever at any significant event — she wasn't there in the crowd. Her corner was empty. Where there would have been cheers, there was silence. She would have been standing beside Kevin at that precise moment, but this was the beginning of a new normal. She wasn't late. She was gone. No more pictures taken by a proud Mama Bear. No more waves or winks or "I see you's." No more embarrassing shouts of "...that's my boy!..." or eager eye-contact. The scene felt noticeably bleak and colorless.

These had been the Zacchaeus moments — to be found and addressed in the whole crowd. Like the Samaritan woman at the well, known and seen. Like the unruly youngsters pressing toward Jesus through resistant adults who are told "Do not hinder them, let them come!" "Not even a sparrow falls to the ground without the Father's care." "His eye is on the sparrow, and I know He watches me." Scripture describes many crowds — the crowds escaping Egypt, the crowds of grieving townspeople, the crowds following the radical carpenter-teacher, the crowds of witnesses cheering us on in our faith.

It's different to step up to the dusty home plate knowing Mom's eye is on you. Different, than, say, getting dropped off and waiting to get picked up when the

game is over. It's different to scan a crowd, locate your crush, and pause —
there he is — and he's already been looking at you, too. It's different when
someone's face lights up in a blurring and greying hoard. I learned from my
mom — in the most comforting, reassuring way — that I am not lost in the
shuffle; someone really sees me. Her eye upon me only heightens my
understanding of the Father's care. Being seen is being known. Being known
is being loved.

God sees and He's happy to see. And He doesn't just "look at" me, He has
education and knowledge, love and acceptance, and He knows. "Nothing in all
creation is hidden from God's sight. Everything is uncovered and laid bare
before His eyes…" Behind and before, above and beyond, here and now. He
has emotional responses to what tickles Him, hurts Him on my behalf, and
excites Him. He is very present and very aware. He's like a mom on a bench in
front of a waterslide, or watching from blue stackable seats as the Pre-K class
marches to the front of the room for "a special song."

Now that I know someone, who has traveled from one world to the next, my
mind has exploded with what the next world might be like. So many creative
possibilities. One scene I anticipate the most: The Arrival. It'll be the next time
she's in the crowd. The King's throne and the Lamb upon it will be front and
center, and I doubt I will have to look for His face. But I've never been in a
crowd of millions, perhaps billions, before. I assume that the people I know
will look different than when I last saw them, but will be immediately and
wonderfully recognizable. I assume there will be angels. Since it's heaven,
after all.

I imagine the crowds won't only be standing flat on the ground. With three-
dimensional, stacked-magic I envision crowds layered as far back in every

direction as the eye can see, but as far up and ahead, too. And she'll be there. It can only be a sensational experience arriving in heaven, with the ability to be awe-struck but also to soak up every bit of wonder and joy. No distraction or disappointment or social-anxiety. No need to manage or lower expectations. Just uninhibited pleasure in every form, with capacity for the first time to feel it all completely without a trace of inhibition. No making fish-faces to avoid smiling.

I imagine what it will be like to feel her again, to scan the faces and find her — already waving to me. I imagine that glowing face I grew to know so well through 25 years of life, and then I marvel as I try to picture how much more magnetic and comforting such a face will be on the One who made me and loved me first: "Well done, good and faithful servant! Come and share your Master's happiness!"

***

This book is about the woman who saw and knew me best for 25 years. Gratefully, I was able to watch her and even now in her absence I have only learned more about her. This is about her life story, and mine as her child. Some of our favorite family stories and some of my small personal tales are written here. These stories have been my teacher; God in her. This book is about my realization that, while there is a specific sort of gray that appears after loss, God has a life-giving, important way of bringing color back: remembering. The memories I carry in my heart, and share with you now, have made all the difference. I hope the woman my mom was — and who she was to me — gives you worthy things to think about (because thinking is just good), makes you feel not-so-crazy, and reminds you how specifically seen and cared for you are in earth's great crowd.

2. THE FAMILY

"I'm writing this in part to tell you that if you ever wonder what you've done in your life, and everyone does wonder sooner or later, you have been God's grace to me, a miracle, something more than a miracle. If only I had the words to tell you."

— Marilynne Robinson

I went to an excellent private school for a few years of my life, and in elementary grades I remember attending the "Creative Writing Workshops" the school hosted. We learned about the "sandwich" of good writing: the opening paragraphs and concluding paragraphs are the bread that hold everything together. In between is the meat of the story, enhanced by the exotic condiments or additions of lettuce and tomato and whatever else you like on your own sandwich. At one of these workshops I was introduced to the concept of a thesis statement and told that if, for example, you are writing about butterflies you never say, "Now I am going to tell you about butterflies." Or if you're writing about a clumsy, nerdy girl named Sofia Maria you never say, "I am going to tell you a story about a clumsy, nerdy girl named Sofia Maria." Instead, you just tell the story and make the readers see and feel the fluttering wings or the nerdy-clumsiness.

Sorry, writing teachers, I think you did a great job. I'd like to introduce you, readers, to a nutshell version of my family before I get too far into this. You'll learn more nuance to them as this unfolds, but we are a crowded family-photo and I want you to know more than just names. You really can't know my mom, or me, without knowing them too. So! I am going to tell you about the members of my family!

***

Alan Harold is our father. He doesn't like either of his names or watermelon with feta cheese on it. Other than that, I think he likes or loves every other food (It was one of the things my mom appreciated most about him: he wasn't a picky eater and he truly enjoyed meals. They loved to eat together.) My friends have taken to calling him Big Al, but I don't think we've ever said that to his face. He is a broad-shouldered, six-foot-something, Italian-German-Irish New Yorker without an accent. He has one brown eye and one green eye. His hair was ink black until it started to pepper but the grey looks better than he thinks it does. He tans easily, thanks to an olive complexion that I'm assuming came from the Rigusa side of the family.

They came to Ellis Island straight from their homeland a few generations ago. My dad's grandmother was Lena, and his mom was Suzanne Carol (which is a happy coincidence because my mom was named Suzanne by her mother, Carol.) If you ever have a chance to eat one of Grandma Sue's full-fledge pasta and garlic meals, don't pass it up. It does not get better than her home cooking. My dad's father was named George, but he was known as "Dirt" around town ("If that tells you anything about him," my dad would say.) At the very end of his life he was transformed — literally overnight — by the grace of God, and was attached to the Catholic faith. But even before his conversion, Grandpa George was the reason my dad understood what "unconditional love" was. No one loved my dad like his dad. I won't go into the details of the family history, but let's just say that it is a little messy on that side.

Dad came from loaded pasts, and he himself has a loaded past. He, like his father, was changed nearly overnight by one of the most distinct "come to Jesus" stories I've ever heard. He who was once the opposite of a devoted, faithful husband and father became a devoted, faithful husband and father. Dad was the star athlete in high school and played football in college ("...But I could have played baseball, too."). He has a master's degree and published his own book of poetry in his 20's. I once caught him, vacuum in hand, crying, while watching ballet on PBS during a Saturday afternoon clean. His favorite movies are *The Notebook* and *Pride and Prejudice* (both versions) and he probably watches each a dozen times a year. He constantly quotes them in normal conversation too. The day after I got engaged, he carried on washing dishes most of the morning, while Mom and the kids and my new fiancé gathered around the living room to tell stories. When he was done he came over, gave me a soft side-hug and pat (a big deal for his not-physically-affectionate-self) and said "Well, congratulations." "Thanks, Dad." "I cannot believe that anyone can deserve you, " he continued, "but it appears I am over-ruled." Daaaad.

He is truly as soft as he is hard. He is an intimidating presence if you don't know him; and, well, can sometimes be intimidating if you do. He coached for many years and only kicked a chair once. His players remember his classic move: the one on his hands and knees, leaning forward, smacking the court with his hand — like a baby trying to figure out how to crawl, instructing furiously. But he is also remembered for driving the team bus to a grocery store after a big win, letting us loose to shop for dinner (we came back with steaks, fries, and ice cream), taking the bus to our home, and at 10:00 pm cooking us a feast. Or turning on Enya during practice warm-ups, because it soothed him. Or sitting us down and earnestly unpacking for a dozen 16 year old girls, that we aren't to be "Valentine's Day athletes." He drew the comparison of a husband who does something elaborate and special on Valentine's Day, versus a husband who is diligent, serving, and detailed year-round. "You don't get to show up at a championship and suddenly become champions. You become a champion right here, at 7:30 pm on a Thursday night, with no crowds, and no ref, and no buzzer — touching every line, sprinting through every drill, not cutting corners. Every day, you show up. And that is a life lesson. It's all the small things that get you to the big ones. You don't become a good spouse one day a year, and you don't become a good basketball player one day a year either."

He's extreme, blunt, and aggressive and he's thoughtful, generous, and warm. He's brilliant and strategic and thrives in every professional role he has pursued. He's competitive and known for turning a simple game of HORSE or poker or tag into a multilevel tournament event. Some of my most vibrant childhood memories are Saturday mornings with him. For years he would pack us all up, leaving Mom to have some quiet sleep to herself. We'd raid either McDonald's or a gas station for crappy, salty, delicious breakfasts and he'd take us to a park to play with us. He was The Mulch Monster or The Pool Dragon, and he'd invent elaborate rules and point systems, and we'd squeal as he made chase. Friday nights, after our school week and his work week, he'd put us to bed and weave his "famous" Special Stories that he made up on the fly and could go on for an hour. He's gruff, don't get me wrong, but he's complex and wonderful and crazy and opinionated and strong and good. He's Big Al and he tells us all the time that we seven kids are his best friends. He's ours, too.

***

Mom, well, you're going to hear a lot about her; but I'll place her in the family tree so you have a foundation. Suzanne Lee was born to Richard and Carol: two tall, classic beauties, in Orange County, California. She was their second child, but their first was a little boy named Ricky who died when he was 10 days old. He had an undetected, but treatable, heart condition. Back in that generation people didn't wear loss and pain on their sleeves the way our millennial generation has learned to do. Mom didn't know much about Ricky. After her mother died, she found a box with a few of his things.

Mom was blonde-haired, blue-eyed, and the pictures of her late 1950's childhood look as darling, perfect, and dreamy as any idyllic image you might have of that time period. Lipstick, well-made feminine dresses, head scarves, timeless cars, buckle Mary Jane's, curled coifs, men in ties and suits, manicured lawns. Her father was a quiet, emotionally-distant, steady banker and her mother was the heartbeat of the family with her joy, creativity, warmth, and welcoming attitude. Mom's memories of her child-hood match the rosy-filtered photos.

My mom and her mom were lifelong best friends and had an especial bond. Mom had two younger sisters, Pam and Lynda, and a baby brother, Scott, 12 years later. They have all had good relationships with each other overall, and are a loving family unit. She had one set of grandparents who lived in an orange grove, and another set who lived nearby. Their home was one block from the elementary school, and there are friends she made during those years who still live on that street today. In fact, the house they were raised in is the house Aunt Pam lives in today. Being there sparks a treasure trove of memories. They went to church on Sunday mornings and Wednesday nights. They played in the pool and Lake Tahoe during the summer, and went sledding and skiing during the winter. Disneyland held a high place in their family culture, as did camping in earthly wonders like Yosemite and Yellowstone.

Mom graduated from high school at 17 and was planning to be married by 19 or 20. College came and went, and she was "still single." She found a job easily with her nursing degree and after a few years decided to join the Army. She traveled often and eventually ended up moving to Washington DC to work at

Walter Reed Memorial Hospital. She saw the world, served others by babysitting and making wedding cakes and bringing meatballs to church events and going on some YWAM (Youth With A Mission) trips. She didn't get married in her twenties. But just after her 30th birthday she and my dad become Mr. and Mrs. She hoped to have four kids, but was "worried" that getting such a late start would mean a smaller family than she had always imagined. (So, no, they did not plan on having seven kids.) She loved being a mother more than anything else in the world, and I guess I'll tie this off here, since the rest of this book carries on from there.

***

On to me! I am Alan and Sue's first child. They were not planning it, but within weeks of their wedding I was alive inside my mother. They didn't find out the gender but my mom was sure I was a boy. They called me "Baby Moses" (but no one can remember where that nickname came from). While Mom was pregnant with me, a church friend was praying for us at a home group meeting and felt very strongly that I would "hear the voice of the Lord at a young age." They named me Kristen, in part because it means "Follower of the Lord." My middle name, Leigh, was after my mom's middle name but she changed the spelling because she thought it was prettier. It means "sheltered in the meadow."

I memorized Psalm 23 in first grade and the line "He makes me lie down in green pastures, He leads me beside quiet waters" was a verse Mom spoke and prayed over me often. When I was two years old I approached my parents, asking about Jesus living in my heart. We said a very simple prayer in the living room; but both my parents kind of assumed this was just a "good direction" but not necessarily the real thing. However, in the following days, weeks, and then years, they would both say that that evening was a turning point in me. I don't remember it, but apparently there was a softness, teachability, and change that was clear and lasting. Today I have in my possession Mom's prayer journal about me during those tiny years, and I would grab this treasure if the house were on fire. Mom and I were buddies. I felt more like her friend than someone under her authority most of the time (until I acted that out and, whoa, could she swiftly offer some clarifications).

I went to private school until third grade, when Mom pulled me out to homeschool — mostly so we could spend more time together. I was homeschooled for nearly the rest of my education. I always played sports and took outside classes, so I was never home for all my subjects. I started playing soccer that third grade year, I think mostly in my parent's effort to make sure I still had friends. Basketball came into my life in sixth grade and it was my favorite, but I played both sports through high school graduation and coached both afterwards. Mom was my biggest cheerleader.

When I started to think about my life after high school graduation, a photography career came more and more into the picture. Dad was my "constructive critic" while Moms's calling was to lavish praise on me. I never went to college. I worked three or four part time jobs while launching my business. I lived on my own for two years before I married my dear Caleb, who actually reminds me so much of Mom. She gave me her love and attention and affection easily. She made me feel special. I'm a little more like my dad in personality, but she really shaped me when it came to the desire to "make a memory" and to have "the little things" be noticed, special, and important. But, again, I have a lot more to share regarding her influence on me so...on to the next Snyder baby.

***

Timmy Tiger. He's a book all his own. When Mom was pregnant with him, nine months after I was born, she was driving and heard an audible, loud voice behind her say "His name is Timothy." She turned around sure someone was in the backseat of the car. But she was alone. She didn't know the gender for this child either, but assumed after the supernatural-voice experience he was indeed a boy. His middle name is Alan, carrying his father's first name.

When Mom was in labor with Tim there were complications. My dad describes it by saying: "With you, it went just like the books say it will. Everything worked and it was incredible. We were first-time parents and had no idea what we were getting into, but it was text book. And we thought 'Wow! This is great!' But with Timmy nothing went like it was supposed to." Dad started to panic a bit in the delivery drama, so he stepped outside briefly to pray and gather his thoughts. I kind of feel like I'm making my family sound like these eye-rolling, ridiculous Christians who keep "hearing things from heaven" and are whack-jobs. We aren't, I promise. These stories were as surreal and crazy to them then as they might sound to you now. But as my dad was praying he felt a very distinct prophetic image overwhelm him. The picture was of the devil with his hands wrapped around the neck of Tim. He heard God speak "Like you've labored in the natural, you will also labor spiritually for Tim. And just as the cord is wrapped around his neck twice, Satan's hands will be wrapped around his neck. But as he will be delivered completely in the natural, he will also be delivered spiritually." After some terrifying moments, Tim was born strangled and purple, but he was alive and quickly thriving.

They took home their robust handsome boy and marveled. When he was 12 days old he was in his crib napping, while my mom putted around the house taking care of chores. A passing thought came to her mind: "Go check on him." He shouldn't have been awake yet, and she hadn't heard anything concerning; but she stopped mid-task to check on him. He was blue and not breathing. She screamed for my grandma to call 911 and she says the Lord just overtook her body and calmly and without hesitation she set his limp body on the floor and began doing CPR until paramedics arrived. It worked and his life was spared once again. The first memory I have of my whole life was that night. I was 18 months old and sitting on the couch while my grandma read Pat The Bunny to me. It was dark outside, when a crowd of people in white clothes came rushing into our house while flashing blue and red ambulance lights bounced across the living room. They left with my mom and baby brother, and when the door closed behind them the siren trailed off until there was silence. "Judy can pat the bunny. Now YOU pat the bunny."

My mom said that my dad took much responsibility for me after these events, but he seemed afraid to bond with Timmy. He was probably subconsciously terrified of losing him, she thought. But over the years they became extremely close. My dad loved him like he'd never loved anyone before. They especially bonded through sports. Tim had natural, impressive abilities and strength; and my dad had proven wisdom and was a master coach. They lived life together talking, teaching, playing, fighting, hoping, and growing. However in early teenage years, Tim really started to fulfill his birth-prophesy. My parents labored for his soul and life for a decade and a half, as he chose self-destruction time and again. Future greatness was at his fingertips, and he had talent to spare. He blew it.

Watching my parents grieve Tim's choices, Tim's pain, and Tim's consequences broke my heart. Mom said that it hurt so bad, partly, because he was the most lovable, sweet little boy. He had sparkling eyes, a completely doofy and infectious sense of humor. He has always been a deep, fascinating thinker, who can talk to anyone about anything and have a marvelous conversation. He was a teddy bear — gone to the dark side.

Two months before Mom died, he checked himself into rehab and came home in time to physically carry his tiny, bony mother to her death bed in his large, strong arms. He wept by her side, singing hymns off-key, and sputtering to

15

songs coming out of the iPhone in his hand. It began a new chapter for him. He's very much in the middle of his story, but he has since become a high school basketball coach and he is more relationally involved with our family than he ever has been in his life. I truly cannot wait to watch this rest of his life play out. He's a special guy with quite a story under his belt and much more story still ahead. The best is very much yet to come.

***

Katelynn Suzanne was their third. Three under three! Their hands, hearts, and laundry baskets were full (and their bank accounts were not). Katie wasn't a calming influence to our already motley crew. She was all passion, feelings, and flair. There is a song by Mama Cass — and a few stanzas specifically — that really remind me of Katie. "You've got to make your own kind of music, sing your own special song! / Make your own kind of music, even if nobody else sings along."

Katie is confusingly complex — even to herself — which can be frustrating to her, and she is highly emotional. Not uncommonly for "feelers," her highs are HIGH and her lows are LOW. As a child, she rode a lot of the high. She was a colorful, hardheaded, affectionate, performing songbird. Mom's pictures show her frequently dressed up in head to toe costumes. One of our family favorites is a snap of her in a long sleeve, red print dress with a floral pink and blue dress over top. She is wearing teal, plastic high heels, ankles crossed like a lady. Smiley-face stickers are stuck all over her own face like cheerful freckles, while she is lying underneath a white lace umbrella, snuggling a jungle cat stuffed animal, sound asleep.

For a couple of years, her preferred uniform was a huge, hot pink t-shirt, little hot pink jean shorts, and a pair of oversized, knee-high, sparkly-black rain boots. She has always been clumsy. Those poor boots didn't help. I once found

Mom looking out a window watching Katie play in the front yard. Mom was laughing so hard she was crying. "That girl just can't stop falling!" She affectionately earned the nickname "monkey" and lived up to it. She was a dangerous turn in the road where you think "I'm surprised more accidents don't happen here." Katie was the first one Mom took to the emergency room for stitches, the first broken bone in the family, the first to fall out of a tree (and missed puncturing her lung by millimeters). She would jump down the stairs wearing robes that were too long and tangled, plastic jewelry clacking away with each bounce. You would always find Katie curled up in some little nook or nest that she had made for herself — on top of couches or behind doors or inside closets or under tables.

She lived in her own world of wonder, and was often misunderstood. As she has grown up, the familiar changes from childhood to adulthood have been hard on Katie. Her younger self had often been slapped in the face with the cold sting of pain; and, as I said, these lows are deep for her. She and I have discussed our occasional, mutual envy: I wish I could feel things more and not be so numb to my emotions, and she wishes she could put mind over matter better and not be so affected by the intense swings. I guess that's why we get to have each other. She's one of the most captivating people I know, who has always had a sixth sense and soft spot with animals and kids.

She has an incredibly strong body to match her tenacious personality. She has stage fright but also inspiring fearlessness. She's the type of person who you meet and connect with only once in your life. No one is "just like Katie." She's an original, mysterious, huge-hearted tiger of a woman. Our natural bents as people have been so different, that it's only been in recent years that we've started to develop a closer friendship. I pushed her away because she wasn't the rule-keeper I valued so much. She couldn't connect with me honestly without feeling trampled.

It's been a huge thing in my life to have begun to earn her trust, but even more: just to know her. Really, slowly — I am learning about this vibrant woman with whom I share bloodlines and so much of life. It's a little scary how you can spend so many years side by side with someone and still be a stranger to their heart. This was my fault and I'm grateful for both the person she is and the person she challenges me to be.

***

Speaking of emotions, Kevin Laurence was born when I was six. He is probably the biggest "feeler" in the family, and he was a mama's boy from day one. My mom treasured having a little guy be expressive and "heart on his sleeve," since my dad and Tim both tended to guard their hearts. Kevin and Katie are similar in passion and imagination.

From a young age, Kevin could be found absorbed in play in a world of his own invention. He was possessed by a couple of characters in particular. There was John and John David, different and distinct construction builders. At four and five years old he would play out of the back of the family station wagon, filling it with both real and plastic tools (like a green and yellow golf caddy and stubby bright blue kid clubs); and he pretended that it was the bed of his pick-up truck. He would saunter out of the vehicle (as either John or John David) with a clipboard and pencil. He'd knock on the front door and ask to speak to the head of the household. My mom would say "I am her." And he'd reply "Wonderful. I just wanted to ask you about your driveway. It appears it needs to be re-paved. Are you interested in a free quote?" Mom would approve the quote and he'd get busy making chicken-scratches and measuring random lines before knocking on the door again. "Okay, ma'am it looks like it will be 23 million 16 dollars." "Oh!" my mom would exclaim, wide eyed, "I'm not sure we can afford that right now! Do you have any deals running?" He'd lift his eyebrows and shift his weight on his little boy hips "As a matter of fact, we do! If you hire us on the spot we can make it happen for six nickels and 8 cents." These sales were always very appealing to Mom's budget and she always accepted the offer. How could you not?

Then there was Sean (he was more of a commercial builder) who always wanted to build an airport in the backyard. And though it might seem crazy, Mom approved these jobs. She could never pass up a good price, even if she didn't need it. What kind of fool fails to purchase an airport for less than a dollar? Not my business-savvy mom. Not her.

Kevin would also play "professional athlete" with vigor. He would set up both of our child-sized basketball hoops and play a semi-final or championship game with himself. But he wasn't just "Michael Jordan" or "Kobe Bryant" in these games. He was the whole team. And the whole opposing team. And even the referees. And the announcers. His mind was buzzing, and he could keep all the scenes together so well. Few sights were more entertaining then Kevin's NBA finals in the basement. He'd call fouls against himself and then flop on the floor and give himself a technical. Then he'd pull himself, the rookie, off the bench. The rookie would fumble the ball thanks to nerves, and the captain (also himself) would give him a pep talk and a firm butt slap. He was a frenetic hamster, running from character to character all over the carpet. It was marvelous. He would even miss the last minute shot at the buzzer to win, and crumple to the ground with his head between his knees.

This enthusiasm and pace of thought has never left the boy. He's all in. Whatever he's in — he is completely there. Mom died during his senior year, just a couple of weeks short of his senior basketball championship game. My dad was the head coach and he was the starting point guard. They played a team in the finals that they had lost to in regular season play. The entire school (and then some) showed up — most of them wearing pink for Mom's memory. The day after my mom died one of the Varsity girl's basketball players died in a tragic accident. The school and the basketball programs were in mourning over these back to back losses.

My dad challenged the boys before the game to win the game not for anyone else: not for Mama Bear, not for Teresa, not for the school, not for him, but for themselves. "This is your team. This is your life. This is thanks to your hard work. Get out there and get your banner." The energy was immeasurably electric. Kevin, and the rest of the boys played the game of their lives and took their banner home. As the final ten seconds ticked away the whole gym was on their feet (even the fans for the opposing team) chanting, "Mama Bear! Mama Bear!" The buzzer sounded, the champions tackled each other, the bleachers emptied, and I've never seen Kevin (or most any of our family) more alive with passion, joy, sadness, and thrill all at once. It was very fitting that our little John-Sean-Kobe-Jordan-mama's-boy grew up to have that moment. And I think it's just the beginning of the out-of-this-world stories he'll bring us.

***

To the emotional intensity of Kevin we now add the logical stability of Michael — child number five and son number three. He is the most stand-alone of us Snyder kids. Generally we are a loud, rowdy, outspoken bunch, with a lot of "boom" when we enter. Mike is different. He goes by "Dude" or "The Dude" by nearly everyone. But my parents called him The Rainman, after the excellent movie and character played by Dustin Hoffman (This was no insensitivity to autism or those who live with it. Dude simply reminded my parents of the movie character, and nurse-mom often wondered — given his unique and particular self — if he might even register on the spectrum.)

He was born with a wit, delivery, OCD, and social-style that was all his own. Our family was, perhaps, known as the messy, noisy, nuts family, and my parents would joke that even as an infant Dude would sit in his highchair with a judgey look on his face like "Heavens. What is the matter with you people?" He would hum whenever he was concentrating. He was always orderly, quiet, and able to take care of himself. He was never a needy person, emotionally or practically. When he was in first grade he made a Christmas Wish List and gave it to my mom. It was written on white computer paper with a green marker and there were five items on the list. Next to each item was a link that he had hand-written for where to find the item online, as well as the price (he researched where the gift could be purchased for the best value).

When he was a toddler he'd loudly sigh, like a disgruntled 50-year-old-woman, as he rolled his eyes and took the trash out on his own initiative, after one of us left it stuffed and overflowing. He's smart and particular and self-sufficient. One night we were watching a family movie. Someone made popcorn, as is usual, and bowls were passed out. Apparently Dude got too much popcorn in his bowl. He didn't want so much popcorn, but he ate it all anyway. It upset him so much that he has never eaten popcorn again (to this day). We didn't find out about this until years later (though we did notice he inexplicably stopped eating the snack). Once he told us, we were like, "Dude?! Why didn't you just eat less?" "Because I always finish what is in my bowl." "But why didn't you just take some out then?" we'd reason. "No, I don't do that. I just wanted less in there to begin with and now it's ruined." Classic him. If someone put syrup on his pancakes before cutting them, he wouldn't eat them. Syrup had to go on after. He makes sure his clothes aren't wrinkled and his shoes aren't dirty. He's an enigma!

He had a very special place in my mom's heart (more on that later) and before she died she was most concerned about him fading to the background of the family. "If Dude ever talks to you, stop what you are doing and listen! He's a deep well and you have to pay attention." It's been meaningful to watch him grow in confidence (sometimes even a little too much), to speak up, and participate the last couple of years. We all agree he's going to be a CEO and the wealthiest of us all someday.

A personal favorite Dude-Tale is a paragraph he wrote for school before Thanksgiving. My mom saved it and showed it to me, but before she did she asked me, "Okay, if you are going to ask a ten year old what they are thankful for, what do they usually say?" I answered, "I don't know? Thankful for their family, their house, their friends, for food?" I wasn't sure where she was going with this. Then she handed me Dude's paper:

"I'm thankful for the sound when you open a Snapple, because it's refreshing and relaxing. I'm thankful for every rainbow I see, because it's a promise from God. I'm thankful for the people who rented our house, because they didn't use all the firewood we left and now we have some to use. I'm thankful for my Call of Duty Modern Warfare games, because they give me some sense to the fact that our country could be attacked and to be grateful for freedom. I'm thankful for today, because I got to experience another great day of my life. I'm thankful for hearing my favorite song come on the radio because it calms me. I'm thankful for the cold side of the pillow because it helps me sleep at night. I'm thankful for every time something is cheaper than I thought it was, because it feels like I'm saving money. I'm thankful for the amount of fries in a Five Guys bag, because it's more than I paid for. I'm thankful for every time I'm early to somewhere, because I don't have to be nervous about being late."

***

(Almost done. Two more!)

Mom had Dude the year she turned 40, so she was very aware that this might be her last baby. She soaked him up like a final gift and tried to prepare her heart for "never again" in this part of her life. She had had five kids in 10 years and in many ways the family just felt right. A couple of girls, a few boys, a decade of bearing children. This was good. Therefore she was shocked, when just a few months after Dude's first birthday, she found out that she was pregnant again. I was at the age where this was just thrilling and I couldn't believe I was going to get to experience one more baby in the family. Mom was due on July 10, 2001 (her third decade in which she delivered a baby since I was born in 1989!), but Mom always delivered late. I had been 11 days past the due date, Tim went 9 days, Katie 5 days, Kevin 12, and Dude was 11 days late. So we settled in for a baby sometime around July 20. Mom went into labor on July 8th and had a very stubborn, responsible, on-time ("because being right on time is late!") little girl, named Shannon Carol — one day early. We were stunned.

Shannon has been competent, in control, and taking care of business ever since. When she was a toddler my dad would say of her, "It sure is hard to run the world, isn't it?" She is very much made to be "the boss" and is really a 30-something wife and mother, balancing home and career with ease, routine, and happiness in a teenager's body. She's got a tough exterior — making her a heckuva soccer player; and a nurturing interior — making her determined to be a nurse or midwife long-term. She and my dad have always had a special bond and we used to call Dad "The Shannon Whisperer." He had a way of reasoning with her and calming her raging-toddler-self like no one else could.

It became evident early on that she is extremely soft-hearted and that part of her steely fortress is protecting what is so delicate inside herself. Once around six years old she was having an infamous tempter tantrum and had locked herself in the bathroom — kicking the walls and knocking soap bottles over. Mom told me to turn on "Amazing Grace" on my iPod and set it outside the bathroom door. I did, and once she heard it she started to yell "NO! TURN THAT OFF." She even tried to stick her fingers under the door and get the iPod so she could turn it off herself, but I moved it faster than she could grab.

Before the second chorus she unlocked the door, sobbing, and draped herself on me apologizing for "being so rotten." "How sweet the sound."

Another time she just burst into tears on a road trip because we were passing car after car and building after building and home after home. "There are people in all these places. People are everywhere!" They are! Mom and Dad, agreed. "It's just so overwhelming," she shared. She felt the bigness of the reality that there are scores of individual people here, with their own lives and own problems and own cares, and man, it hit her heart hard. Like my dad, she can go from one extreme to the other very quickly. The most tough and yet the most tender. I've said before that "I want to be like Shannon when I grow up." She is very much a spirit and strength that we didn't know we needed, without which we cannot imagine our family.

***

And if Shannon was a surprise to the family, then Lauren was blindsiding. When Shannon was six months old, Mom got pregnant with Lauren. Mom would be 43 by her due date. This was unbelievable to her! But she was truly grateful for another "this is actually probably the last one" baby to absorb and love. In came Lauren Catherine, later changed (but not yet legally) to Lauren Chloe (because my parents were naming her after my dad's sister Cathy, who had passed away. But it turns out her real name was Cathleen not Catherine. So after the hubbub they re-named Lauren after my dad's other sister, Chloe.) She came 14 days past her due date and has been late and chillin' ever since.

Lauren seems to have been born happy, with smiling eyes and smiling cheeks. She is one of those people who lights up a room and is just plain like-able. She's also startlingly perceptive, particularly about the nuances of human interaction. If any of us were to grow up to be a stand-up comedian, it would be her. She's not perfect, of course. Poor thing inherited our dad's "neuroses," as he calls them. She's scared of everything and breaks out in a rash when she's especially stressed. We're all proud of her courage, and we all probably wish we were a little more like her when it comes to sweetness. We have a lot of, um, savory in the family.

Mom let her suck her thumb until she was five and sleep in their bed until she was six. She and I talk regularly about favorite meals we've had or meals we dream of having. She's adorably bad at the details and has the best laugh. When she's mad she's stone cold; but we know — and she knows we know — that she's being ridiculous and that it will blow over in a few minutes. When she was little my dad gave her the nickname "Bear Face" because of the pouty scowl that would come over her when she was displeased — much like a displeased little bear. We love this last one in Papa and Mama Bear's pack of cubs. It sounds hokey, but she completes us.

***

We're difficult and hard-thinking people. We're all complex and very intense. We're definitely that family you would see out and about and think "Oh gawd, how do those parents do it?" We don't make having a big family look easy. We don't sweep things under the rug, which can be good; but sometimes that means we have so much mess all out at once, that we don't even know where to begin. We really do love each other. We think we're pretty funny and have interesting things to say. Any one of us can have a really good conversation with any other one. There are some difficult parts of our family history and some things so sweet it seems like heaven touched earth. This is us. She was our Mama Bear. This is the family that was her world.

At her funeral my dad shared that our home was built on the foundation of the Lord, but that it was held up by the I-Beam that was our mother. We were loved and loved each other best through her. Losing her threatened to cause the roof to cave in and the walls to crumble down. My dad exhorted us each at the service to reach up and each hold our part of the weight. Together, he said, we can hold this family up. It has been messier and sadder, in certain ways, than we thought it would be. Children are not supposed to be separated from their parents. It's just not how it's meant to be. Parents aren't supposed to be bad or abusive or sick or die. Children aren't supposed to be left alone or cut off or be sick or die.

It won't be this way forever. There will be a time when families will be whole, and the tear wounds where they were ripped apart will be healed. All of this will just be an old part of a past life. At the same time, it's quite true that "Experience: that most brutal of teachers. But you learn, my God do you learn."(CS Lewis) We've all learned heavily without her. Sometimes we've learned the hard way, and sometimes we've been able to come into an easy grace that is very available. We are closer as a family. Truly. Half of us are adults now. We're thinking out loud, learning to trust each other with our hearts, sharing the sacred place that no one else in the world knows like we do — like the children that lost their mother, Sue Snyder, do.

This is about her, mostly. Maybe it's too soon to write this, but I don't want to forget things. Her closet still smells like her, but it's fading. I don't know what will play out for us in the next decades, but I know what we had with her. As time goes on, I feel like I understand and appreciate her to a greater extent. I wish more and more that I could have one hour with her. Maybe this is my way of having an hour with her. Of letting others have an hour with her. So keep these characters in mind, as I have the honor of spilling the beans and praising the woman who made our lives. We were her family, and she was the sun we orbited.

What Mama Bear Taught Me About...
3. ҒOOD

"I know the look of an apple that is roasting and sizzling on the hearth on a winter's evening, and I know the comfort that comes of eating it hot, along with some sugar and a drench of cream...I know how the nuts taken in conjunction with winter apples, cider, and doughnuts, make old people's tales and old jokes sound fresh and crisp and enchanting."
— Mark Twain

Food is well-loved in our family. As a little girl, when I saw the nightly routine of cabinets being opened, produce taken from the fridge, bowls on the counter, dinner being prepared, I wanted to be a part of the process. I wanted Mom to be pleased with my slicing skills, and I wanted to sneak bites of freshly grated cheese or a noodle from the strainer.

Mom was wonderful about giving us tasks in the kitchen. She rarely said, "No, not today" when the inevitable faces wandered onto the linoleum begging for a roles as sous chefs. She found a way to put us to work (I think she also knew we'd disappear in five minutes more often than not). She found plastic knives in the back of drawers for her Kitchen Team. We mashed away on black olives, salami, turkey, cheese "cubes," cucumbers, and cherry tomatoes for salads. We stirred oil and vinegar, splashing almost like we were in the bathtub. We rounded out meatballs — too big, too small, and once in a while we'd get one just right. We'd sprinkle pepper over a casserole (it's a great use of those bad shakers that barely release!) and parsley flakes onto garlic bread. OH! And there was nothing better than using tiny paint brushes to slop melted butter all over a fresh baguette. We'd lick spoons, splatter sauce, and drop Pillsbury rolls on the floor putting them quickly back on the pan. It was great, inefficient, slow-moving fun.

Through the years, I had a dawning realization: I was getting the "easy jobs." I started to notice that I couldn't dice an onion, knead dough, seamlessly butter bread with a knife, or beat batter until it was smooth. And I didn't like it. I wanted to be just like Mom! I wanted to be able to do it too.

I remember one particular day when the rest of the kids weren't around and I asked Mom if I could help make the salad. She told me this wasn't a normal salad, and that she didn't need any olives or cheese cut. "But you can rinse the lettuce if you want!" "Can I cut the apples?" She paused. "I'm not sure if you know how to cut apples yet." "Can you teach me?" I know (now) that she was contemplating her elementary-school-firstborn with a sharp knife. Is she ready for it? She was processing "This could take a while. Am I ready for it?"

"Yes, I can teach you." So her cruise-control dinner prep braked to a stop while she veered off the freeway to pause at a scenic view. She pulled out a knife with a black handle. It was like the scepter of Xerxes being extended to me. I was ecstatic but trying to keep my cool. She talked me through the proper grip. Golf coaches everywhere would have been impressed. She reviewed the safety rules. Make sure food is the only thing under the knife, not fingers. Don't point the knife towards yourself, always away. Cut down, don't pull up or stab. Be gentle and strong, don't be impulsive or rushed. Curl your nails under your knuckles just in case an accident happens. She gave a few live demonstrations of the best way to do the actually slicing, holding my hand over hers so I could feel the motion properly.

And then she left me to chop some apples. I mean, she was a foot and a half away at the sink de-leafing broccoli, but she didn't hover. We usually chatted during kitchen time, but this was no mindless olive-smashing. I focused and she let me do it by myself. The apple pieces were turning brown by the time I was done. The edges were soggy and the shapes were... eclectic. I didn't make the most of my three apples, either. There was lots of apple "meat" left around the core. And with the proudest, warmest smile Mom scooped my measly fruit pile up into her hands while winking at me. I stood a little straighter as I watched my hard-work be dumped into the finished salad bowl. It was the most beautiful salad I had ever seen. I ate it with pride and felt a glow in my belly when she told the whole family that "Kristen was a huge help tonight! She cut all the apples by herself!"

Mom wanted us to be comfortable in the kitchen. When I started showing interest in cooking, she let me at it -- and lawd did my poor family eat some salty, dried out, over-cooked, oddly-flavored meals (ranch dressing pasta, anyone?!). But it was very important to her that I learned for myself, that I didn't feel overwhelmed and over-criticized, and that I knew I was welcome in the kitchen. I created a lot of mess, waste, and leftovers, but whenever I asked, "Can I make dinner?!" I can't recall a rejection.

She understood the rush of raw turning golden, the sharp smells becoming savory, the feel of tomato seeds and onion along your cuticles, the happiness in presenting a family with the last meal of the day (especially one they scarf down). She made it such a joy to make food because she was so relaxed, patient, and flexible. She lifted the burdens of "That cost a lot of money!," "This kitchen is a WRECK," and other failures from me. She taught me to be creative yet careful. Honestly, she just made it fun.

***

As I'll flesh out later, Mom had a soapbox-mantra. "You have to be flexible — I will not raise you to be a rigid person! You have to be able to adapt and go with the flow!" She must have said "Relax, be fleeeeexible" to at least one of us every single day. Food was a primary topic of flexing.

She wanted us, first, to be able to go anywhere and try (then eat) what was served to us without fuss or fanfare ("It's just one meal. It won't kill you. Be polite and never say 'I don't like _____!' after someone has taken the time to make you something.") Second, she wanted us to learn to develop an appreciation for flavors we weren't used to. She'd always tell me how, as a child, she hated guacamole but as an adult she loved it. "Your taste buds get replaced and your palate can enjoy more complex flavors! Don't give up on something! Always try it again!" She was right. I do love avocado now.

***

"It's frustrating to me to see people using food, instead of relating to it. 'Eating is a chore,' says a friend, and it's not the first time I've heard someone say those words. This utilitarian, eat-because-I-have-to relationship with food is unhealthy at best, and is perhaps a reflection of more serious issues: displacement, non-identification with one's physical self, and a lack of ability to savor life outside of the manufactured world of technology, efficiency, and production. I would argue, even, that it is anti-Christian to have a merely utilitarian relationship to one's food. If God incarnate as the man Jesus made such a point of instituting the sacrament of communion and said that the bread was His body and the wine His blood, food can never again be just something we put in our bodies ('fuel' says that horrible industrialist metaphor) to provide energy for our day. God has eaten with us and made the very act of eating together something that He not only identified with, but made a vital part of how we relate to Him and each other.

Food is a curiosity and a communal art for my family, so it's been a bit amazing
to me to leave home and discover that this is pretty unusual (in middle class
America) today. Most people don't know where their food comes from, don't
know how cook beyond following the directions of a recipe, and don't have much
of a personal relationship to food beyond silencing hunger and supplying
energy. There's no holistic ethos for why we eat and where and how."
–Hannah Ettinger

When we were in the toddler and elementary school years as a family, Mom
had a strict afternoon routine: we always had in-room rest time. "You don't
have to sleep, but you do need to rest." We could play quietly or read books or
go ahead and take that nap. Nine out of ten times, minutes after all our doors
were closed, the smell of nachos on fried beans wafted down the hall —
followed by the "ding!" of the toaster oven. Mom's little treat to herself (she
would put a dollop of sour cream in one corner of the tray, a spoonful of salsa
in another, sliced black olives catty corner, and pickled peppers in the last
space). I crave a small tray of afternoon nachos to this day.

Every year on Thanksgiving we would turn on the Macy's parade and Mom
would set out onion dip and ruffled potato chips, meat-cheese-and-crackers-
tray, and shrimp with cocktail sauce. Every year. These appetizers are as
important and classic to my memories as the mashed potatoes and turkey
dunked in gravy. Christmas breakfast was the same every single year, too. For
most of my life, my birthday dessert was a watermelon sherbet cake from
Friendly's, since I didn't prefer real cake. I can taste the chocolate chip "seeds"
this very moment. We went through a stage of having Chinese take-out for
dinner on Sunday nights in the fall when I was in high school.

My dad took his teams to 3 Brothers Pizza on Rockville Pike after away games
until it closed. We ran through the cold, dark parking lot in black sneakers,
athletic shorts, and puffy mismatched winter jackets to take over the whole

establishment and drip red sauce on the white numbers of our uniforms. When Mom was pregnant she always wanted a certain spicy chicken sandwich from a particular fast food joint.

When my dad's mom comes to town she always makes an enormous pot of sausage-tomato-cream sauce to pour over bowtie pasta. She baby-sits the pot all day long and it shows in the flavors. We planned our timing of getting a churro in Disneyland, always waiting to have one fresh and hot. Mom cycled through making homemade popcorn over the stove or in her air popper, or even just in the microwave, because she knew well that evening TV really isn't as enjoyable without a bowl. One of Mom and Dad's favorite date night spots had artichoke dip "to die for" and she couldn't get over it when the place shut down. Summer officially arriving was nearly always marked by a big bowl of Mom's taco salad for dinner. Though I don't remember them myself, I feel as if I know my grandma's grilled cheese sandwich lunches (with a side of cold pickle) thanks to my mom's detailed descriptions of her favorite childhood lunch.

***

"If we didn't have bodies, we couldn't feel the sun on our faces or smell the earthy, mushroom-y rich smell of the ground right after the rain. If we didn't have bodies, we couldn't wrap our arms around the people we love or taste a perfect tomato right at the height of summer. I don't want to live in a world that's all dry ideas and theorems. Food is one of the ways we acknowledge our humanity, our appetites, our need for nourishment.

And so it may seem trivial or peripheral to some people, but to me, when I'm telling a story, the part about what we ate really does matter."
–Shauna Niequist

Mom was the sort of person that you discussed a meal with. She really read the menu and loved to explore herself into a predicament: "I just don't know what to choose! What are you getting?" Standard meal procedure with her was getting one or two appetizers and two entrees, and sharing them all, so we could both have a little bit of everything we wanted. If we went to someone's house or spent a meal away from her she would never forget to ask what we ate and if it was good. She read cookbooks at the beach, had cooking shows on in the background during the day, and took every opportunity to "grab a bite to eat" — an experience she learned through her own mother.

One time she went to a chain Italian restaurant and had a bad experience with their lobster ravioli. For years after that, every time we went to that restaurant she would pause us, whoever she was with, and say, "I recommend everything they make here, except the lobster ravioli. It's surprisingly bad!" We finally broke down and told her, "We know, Mom! You tell us every time!" She laughed so hard! It tickled her to discover that she warned us so firmly every visit, and that apparently this pasta dish had made a profound impression. The joke endured. Whenever we were figuring out where to eat: "Mom, any ideas on where we can get some amazing lobster ravioli?!"

***

"And on it goes. Christian liberty is illustrated by discussions of meat and wine. New Testament fellowship is described as, 'breaking bread from house to house, they ate their food with glad and sincere hearts.' Hospitality was a centerpiece of New Testament Christian living. I could go on and on. The Bible is full of food. Physical food, spiritual food – God as food, the Word as food, salvation as food, etc. It's everywhere. The essence of our hope is that we all have received an invitation to the most spectacular wedding feast ever prepared..."
–Don Shorey

Mom's number one, dominant side effect in pregnancy was nausea. She was the type who threw up multiple times a day for the first four or five months and then shortened it down to once a day or so until delivery. She was also the type who said throwing up wasn't so bad — it was the nausea that pushed her over the edge.

I remember her crawling up the stairs, to get us all ready for the day, when we were small. She would lay in the hallway and have us bring diapers or clothes or brushes to her. When I was a pre-teen she would send me into the grocery store with a $20 bill and short list of things we needed for dinner, while she hung her head outside the minivan door in the parking lot.

You would think that watching so much sickness and throwing up I would have been prepared for my turn to be pregnant. But no such thing happened. I even had this whimsical little thought that, "Maybe I won't get sick!" In the last three years and change, that Caleb and I have been married, I've been pregnant three times (one ending in miscarriage). Totaled up, I've spent close to a year in the "miserably nauseous" stage.

In pregnancy alone my mom spent four and a half years hugging toilets. But thanks to chemotherapy treatments she lived nauseous and vomiting for about seven years of her life. I would describe her as a robot — this incredible creature who could press on no matter what she felt — but that would minimize her strength because robots don't feel. She was a warrior. I was impressed with her back then, but I had no idea what she was actually going through. Now that I've tasted a small sip of her pain, I throw-up my hands, wave my white flag, and bow before her. I have NO idea how she did it. Did life. Did mothering. Did loving. Did not-complaining. Without pageantry or emotional breakdowns, she endured quietly.

We had to ask her how she was feeling to know, because she never told us herself. I even became prematurely self-righteous about "physical suffering" because I repeated what I heard my mom say, though I personally had no proven experience myself. When it was my turn to go for a little ride, I fell apart. I do not handle physical misery well. I'm neither graceful nor selfless when I'm pushed that hard. I cry, I moan, I whimper, I hang on for ever-loving-dear life and look about as bad as I feel. Mom wasn't like this. Mom was stoic, calm, and measured. I come unhinged.

Among the many woes of spinning, throbbing, sour, immobilized sickness is one I had never taken into account: the battle to enjoy (or even just use) food. Coming from such a "food-positive" family culture, I found myself a bit shocked at how hard and un-fun eating was while experiencing long-term nausea. I mentioned this newfound predicament to Mom and she smiled. "It is sad to lose the love of food." MOM. Yes! It is! How come you've never made a big deal about this?! She laughed at her poor, pale daughter. "It'll be even better than you remember when you can enjoy it again. It's one of the few perks to being so sick." In her wise conversation moment she talked about how loss of something you love creates a capacity to enjoy it even more when reunited with said love. She lived in that place. Suffering or losing was a holding pattern before things became so much better — or at least seemed that way.

***

Five months before she died we took our last family vacation. Caleb and I had free airline vouchers from a mix-up during our honeymoon, and they needed to be used within the year. So we HAD to take a trip somewhere, of course! It seemed like the perfect excuse to get him to the west coast for the first time, and it would be our first trip as a family of three.

Once Mom heard that her grandson was taking his maiden voyage to her home state of California — and Disneyland — she had to come too. After a few afternoons of tracking down credit card points, getting kids to re-arrange work schedules, and touching base with old friends, Mom had plane tickets for the rest of the family.

Our first stop was in Anaheim and all of Mom's siblings met us there, too. In our heart of hearts we knew this was Mom's last Disney visit. She looked beautiful and was glowing with peaceful happiness all day long. If snarky comments or childish arguments broke out during that day she just turned the other way and tuned it out. She wanted to walk as long as she could without using the wheelchair, but she had to give in sooner than she wished. Her lymphedema arm was swelling badly in the heat.

I remember, in the late afternoon, when shadows lean and heads are traced in orange-yellow, we sat in New Orleans Square while waiting for a batch of kids to get off a ride. Mom treated herself to a churro. She sat on a sea-green, ornate iron bench and a small spindle of steam rose from the fried sugar-dough, like a candle had just been blown out. She breathed in, closed her eyes, took a bite, and didn't open her eyes until the food was gone. Foot-tapping, Big Easy jazz played through secret speakers. The horns were chirpy. A large, white river boat rang its bell and snorted its smoke. Children and grown adults wearing fanciful hats and bright colors passed like white noise. She looked to the right for a long pause and to the left lingeringly before taking another bite.

"You having a good time, Mom?" "I'm having a wonderful time." By that trip she had learned. She knew about savoring — not as a cute quote for a chalkboard, but as a way of life. She knew the gift "being able to enjoy" was. If she was able, she was going to taste. If she was able, her senses were going to be used to their brink. There was no time to point out the discomforts or bothers, there was barely enough time for the pleasures.

Two nights later on the same trip she could only manage three bites of chips and guacamole at our family dinner overlooking the ocean, sunset, and palm trees in Santa Monica. All the boys laughed so hard that night. I remember it well. The girls took turns holding Rowdy and taking pictures. Mom sat with us as long as she could, until she needed to go back to her hotel room to throw up and lay down. "Just a few more minutes." "Mom, I can walk you up there now...I don't want you to be miserable." "No, no. Not yet. I'll go when I have to. I have a few more minutes in me."

It was a couple of weeks after returning from that grand, California vacation that Mom cooked an important meal. I'm glad we remember it because for the most part it was a very unmemorable evening. Sunny, early autumn. Teenagers passing through with soccer cleats and backpacks. Dishes in the sink and papers spread out over the counter. Mom had been resting most of the day, but she came down and made creamy bell-pepper chicken pasta — a recipe from the Creme de Colorado cookbook that her best friend, Tracy, had given her almost a decade before. We ate it with Caesar salad. Dad did the dishes when we were done, while watching Seinfeld in the background. And Mom never made a meal for the family ever again.

***

In her final months Mom lost too much weight, which is what happens when your body is shutting down. I remember going to her last chemotherapy appointment with her. It was the nurses. They were usually very engaging and chatty, but they wouldn't look at Mom or me in the eyes. They were polite, but quiet. They didn't say "hi" to Rowdy or ask Mom about basketball season. My stomach dropped and I knew they knew. Our after-appointment lunches turned into after-appointment-Kristen-run-in-to-the-stores-while-Mom-waits-in-the-van events. She nibbled and couldn't feast. She talked about how good the food is going to taste in heaven — how it'll never make her feel sick and never come back up.

The day before she died we tried to ask her if there was anything she wanted to eat and she couldn't come up with a single thing. "I'll go anywhere. If you can think of anything I'll go get it." "I'm sorry, I just really can't." I made her a plate of about ten small slices of options: apples, cheese, carrots, crackers, and the like. The plate was left untouched. When her friend and hospice nurse came that evening she told me not to worry about keeping her fed. "Her body knows what to do, and our job at this point is to make sure she's comfortable, not nourished. If she asks to eat, offer her whatever she wants, but she probably won't. Her body knows it doesn't need food anymore. There's a phrase we use that's helpful: 'I'm not dying because I'm not eating, I'm not eating because I'm dying.'"

"We ate well and cheaply and drank well and cheaply and slept well and warm together and loved each other." (Ernest Hemingway) You don't need food to die, you need food to live. Mom showed me this. It was never about cumin with cilantro, or something hot and also creamy, or citrus and poultry combinations. It was about life. About being alive. It was about joy. Stabbing joy with a fork. Cupping joy with a spoon. Physically slicing through joy. Smelling joy. Fistfuls of joy. Joy melting and running down the soft part of your forearm. Awaiting joy, making joy, passing joy around on a plate, and offering for others to share it. To take it and put it inside themselves. Literally breathe it in and swallow it so it travels deep inside of you. Crumbs of joy left on floors, in beds, on clothes, in cars. Joy staining your shirt. Joy spilling on your table. Joy bubbling. Joy steaming. Joy warming. Joy cooling. We could have been plants and only needed some water and a certain kind of air. We could have been rocks and needed nothing. But we eat, because we are so very alive. What a joy.

A FEW OF MOM'S FAVORITE RECIPES

FRIED BEAN NAPTIME TREAT
1 serving

INGREDIENTS 2 corn tortillas • 1 can of favorite refried beans • ½ cup pepper jack cheese (or, you know, any cheese) • a handful of coleslaw cabbage • fresh cilantro • ¼ cup of Green Pepper Tabasco Sauce • 2 tablespoons butter or oil • ½ teaspoon chopped garlic • ½ teaspoon salt

Turn on stove and add butter or oil to melt in pan over heat. In the meantime, spread a couple spoonfuls of beans onto one tortilla. Sprinkle with cheese. Add the second tortilla to the top. Once pan is hot and "sizzles" with a flick of water, add garlic. Let cook for a minute or two. Remove garlic (or, as my mom would do: push it to the side of the pan). Add tortilla stack. Cook on each side for 2-3 minutes, sprinkling a bit of salt on each side once done cooking. Remove from heat when crispy. As it cools, mix cabbage, cilantro, and Tabasco sauce. Put slaw atop tortillas, and feast!

THANKSGIVING DAY ONION DIP

INGREDIENTS 2 yellow onions • 4 tablespoons unsalted butter • 1/4 cup
vegetable oil • 1/4 teaspoon ground cayenne pepper • 1 teaspoon Kosher
salt • 1/2 teaspoon freshly ground black pepper • 4 ounces cream cheese, at
room temperature • 1/2 cup sour cream • 1/2 cup good mayonnaise

Cut the onions in half and then slice them into 1/8-inch thick half-rounds.
(You will have about 3 cups of onions.) Heat the butter and oil in a large sauté
pan over medium heat. Add the onions, cayenne, salt, and pepper and sauté
for 10 minutes. Reduce the heat to medium-low and cook, stirring
occasionally, for 20 more minutes until the onions are browned and
caramelized. Allow the onions to cool.
Place the cream cheese, sour cream and mayonnaise in the bowl of an electric
mixer fitted with the paddle attachment and beat until smooth. Add the
onions and mix well. Taste for seasonings. Serve at room temperature.

Recipe courtesy of Ina Garten from The Barefoot Contessa Cookbook (1999)

CHICKEN BELL PEPPER PASTA
6-8 servings

INGREDIENTS 2 pounds boneless chicken breast • 3 tablespoons unsalted butter • 1 medium red bell pepper, cut into julienne strips • 1 medium yellow bell pepper, cut in julienne strips • ½ cup dry white wine • ½ cup chicken broth • 2 cups heavy cream • 1 cup sliced mushrooms • 2 tablespoons butter • ½ teaspoon salt • ¾ cup freshly grated Parmesan cheese • ¼ cup minced fresh basil • 12 ounces spinach fettuccine, cooked al dente and drained MARINADE ½ cup olive oil • ¼ cup minced fresh basil • 3 tablespoons fresh lemon juice • 1 tablespoon crushed red pepper flakes • 2 teaspoons minced garlic

In a shallow dish, mix marinade ingredients. Add chicken, turning to coat. Cover and refrigerate overnight if possible. In large skillet, melt 3 tablespoons butter and sauté peppers for 2 minutes. Remove peppers; reserve. Stir in wine and chicken broth. Increase heat to high and boil until sauce is reduced to 2 tablespoons, about 5 minutes. Add cream and cook until sauce is reduced by half, about 4 minutes. In another skillet, sauté mushrooms in 2 tablespoons butter over medium-high heat until slightly browned. Add peppers, cream sauce. and salt. Drain chicken, discarding marinade. Broil chicken 4 inches from heat, turning once, cooking until tender and juices run clear. (Chicken may also be grilled.) Discard skin and cut chicken into ½-inch strips. Stir Parmesan and ¼ cup basil into heated pepper sauce. On heated platter, arrange chicken attractively on top of warm fettuccine and pour sauce over top to cover. Serve immediately.

Recipe courtesy of the Creme de Colorado Cookbook (1987)

What Mama Bear Taught Me About…
4. BODIES

"You do not have to walk on your knees for a hundred miles through the desert, repenting…"
— Mary Oliver

Myrtle Beach was the first stop on our family road-trip. Charleston, South Carolina, plains in Georgia, New Orleans, and a ride through Nashville were all up ahead. Our hotel was a kitschy, rickety, damp, beachside paradise. Mom had originally booked a place to stay a few blocks into town, but we drove by this 'masterpiece' and our wonder-child eyes grew three sizes. Neon blue siding, plastic pink flamingos, faded twinkle lights lazily hugging all bushes and trees, lime green staircases, sparkly orange lettering, rowboats hanging off the roof. It looked like a dumpy, shore version of Donald Duck's home. "PLEASE, Dad, PLEASE can we stay at THAT hotel?!" One quick glance with Mom, a head nod, and he made the left turn into the parking lot. "I'm just going to check the prices. Don't get your hopes up. Wait here in the car—don't get out of your seat-belts—I'll be right back."

At the front desk he sealed a thrifty deal and came out with room keys in his hands. They were golden tickets wrapping a chocolate bar to us. And the perfect beginning to a family vacation. I don't know what your family cared about when traveling, but mine had tunnel vision: a hotel with a swimming pool. We obliviously slept in the dingiest rooms, with the thinnest walls and lumpiest beds; but all that mattered was that we could swim until midnight and swim again before breakfast. So we slept with visions of sugar plums and cannon balls dancing g in our heads. Our electric beach shack had a pool: but not just any old pool. It had a pool facing the ocean, about a football field away from the waves. Does it get better than that? We already had our swimsuits on under our clothes.

Within minutes of arriving, our screeches echoed through the courtyard and we had flooded the pool-deck — thanks to our diving contests. Mom came down to keep an eye on us. She even took her cover-up off and jumped in the pool with us for a bit. Wet hair, no make-up, glasses, and healthy but soft belly in a swim suit. Shannon was a toddler at the time, and she wanted Mom to hold her out of the water. Mom wrapped her in a towel and found a sunny patch to lie in a flimsy, plastic recliner for some Vitamin D therapy.

This summer was among the first that I felt very uncomfortable in a swimsuit. Before I ran down to the pool, I had to find my dad's razor in his suitcase and "clean up" my arm pits. The summer before I didn't even know about arm-pit hair. This summer my suit needed a built-in bra. Last summer I was just a child. This summer I had secret stretch marks on my thighs. Last summer I had secret stashes of quarters to get more out of the vending machine. This summer I thought about what I ate for lunch and if it would make me look (or be!) bloated. I found myself not enjoying the pool-play nearly as much as I had in the past. I felt like covering up. I didn't want to get out of the water and jump back into the pool. I was aware of how a suit suctions to the area around your belly button when you move from water to dry land (and no amount of " sucking in" can fix it). This summer I thought about my waist and size. Last summer I thought about making the biggest splash possible.

Eventually I gave in to my insecurities and wrapped up in a towel to hide. I pulled a chair next to Mom and Shannon, closed my eyes, and focused on getting a swoon-worthy tan. While I laid there I overheard Shannon squawking to Mom, "squash squash SQUISHY!" while she kneaded Mom's thighs and midsection. Mom laughed and said "Yes, it is squishy!" While her sixth child happily cuddled and paddled her soft spots, Mom laughed and played too. Then Mom said, "This...this right here came from YOU!" and she pinched up a roll from her waist, showing it to Shannon. "This Little Pig"-style, she pulled up a second roll "And this little squish came from Mikey." A third: "This one is from Kevin, while this one is from Katie!" Shannon held onto the pliable skin as Mom continued. "THIS one is from Timmy Tiger, and this one was the very beginning thanks to Kristen! But do you know where this one came from?" She squeezed a lump up near her ribcage with both hands. Shannon didn't say anything, but just looked at her. "THIS one is from pizza! Yum yum yum yum!"

My toned, athletic, 12-year-old body was in perfectly lovely condition. Perhaps even stunning condition. I played sports year-round and was very healthy. I wasn't overweight, but my short waist and large ribs meant I didn't have a flat stomach -- I never have. I'm squat and boxy on top, just like my mom. As I hid my beautiful body, I was shocked at my mother's boldness. Wasn't she embarrassed? I mean, I did think she was pretty, but how could she talk about and point out and...play with?! her "fat" like that? (Keep in mind: my mom was a small lady. Even at her heaviest she was only a few pounds from her ideal weight. She was no swimsuit model, but she was healthy and strong and petite and very average. It's just that you don't have seven children in your thirties and forties without some "badges of honor.") I truly could not understand her casual confidence and her joy. She wasn't hiding. She was happy and she had belly rolls — for everyone to see! — in her swimsuit.

***

Only a few short years after that pool-side scene, cancer tumored into our lives. She likely already had cancer that day in the pool, long before we even knew about it. Mom's body became a battleground of epic, life-threatening proportions. Watching mama lose her hair, swell due to steroids, have a breast cut off, shrink due to nausea, and eventually "become loosed to death" redefined body-worth to me.

Her sweet ways of coping with baldness (like wearing a rainbow clown wig at my brother's surprise party), her gratitude for the smallest health perks ("I never thought I'd get into these jeans again! Watch out, because you have yourself a hot mama!") and her playful remarks about herself were life-changing for this daughter. She shook her head and made acne-infomercial jokes when one medicine made her face break out. She laughed harder than anyone about her "electrocution hair" (after she lost her hair for the third time, it grew back in light blonde and grey, and it stood STRAIGHT up. It didn't "fall" onto her head — it was like shoots of grass that were just vertical). She found it exciting that her fingers were finally small enough to fit back into her engagement ring. There was always something good or nonsensical or something to be grateful for. Once after she threw up her lunch she commented, "I'm so glad I felt well enough to eat it! It was delicious!"

The woman encased in this ever-changing, five-foot-few-inch body was spectacular. From lumpiness to boniness, she was a dangerously beautiful person. I witnessed it for myself. I saw her sinking eyes, ships at evening sea, grow darker and darker. I heard the grassy, gurgly fight to breathe. I watched her thick rib cage rise and fall for the last time. I wiped drool from her good chin — "If I could have had a different nose I would have been okay with that, but I have a good chin. I like my chin." I smelled the sharp stench of leaving this world. I escorted a now pre-teen Shannon up to Mom's death bed, to say goodbye to her body. I cried as Shannon carefully wrapped herself around

Mom's skeletal waist, held her, and whispered "I miss you already." I know angels filled the room and my mother was never more horribly beautiful.

***

At one of the final chemo appointments Mom and I were talking about bodies. We love to people watch, and we point out any and every thing that interests us. Fashion sense, personality, owners who look like their dogs. One patient packed up to leave as we were settling into the waiting room. Once the patient was gone Mom said, "There is a story behind that forehead." I laughed carefully, even though the woman had left. "I'm serious! I wonder who she got that from? Her father or her mother? Or a grandparent? Someone gave that to her, and that person is a part of her face forever. I really found it beautiful!" I told her that she was getting quite profound at the end. She responded, "I just like people's imperfections or weird features. It's makes them more interesting to me. But yes, I am very profound."

Sitting in that same waiting room I was talking to her about my after-baby-body. I had no idea how to dress it, or how to feel in it. I had never been more proud of myself and grateful for health, but I had also never felt so foreign in my own skin. At one point I said "Thank God I'm not married to a man who cares about how flat my stomach is. He even swears he thinks my stretch marks are beautiful. He's so grateful they gave us Rowdy." Mom's eyes welled up and she said "I hope you listen to him. Please listen."

Imperfect, floppy, pointy, shapely, funny, weird features are everywhere. On all of us. Now when I see them on others I love them. I'm in a coffee shop in Santa Barbara, typing at a corner table next to a large, arched window. The barista leaving work has short, chubby legs; they make him extra stuffed-animal-like and endearing. He has a friendly tone of voice too. A lady waiting in line has red arm-dimples. I have matching red arm-dimples. Her hair is curly — from her mom? Or her dad? Or her great-grandmother in Finland? A woman in her 60's, I presume, is on crutches outside my window. Hopefully not a severe injury. A misstep on the stairs? A fall off a chair in the kitchen? She has a wedding band on, and two hearts on her necklace. Her two children? She has a soft pouch under her faint blue eyelet top. Her hair is braided and thick. All of these people are lovely to me. I could stare for a while.

Oh! Computer nerd, with Vegas sunglasses, wrinkly plaid shirt, Birkenstocks, and cargo shorts just came in! He has small ankles and copper hair. His shirt is too short (probably in the dryer for too long). His hair stands up high (naturally? Or a blow-dryer and gel? I guess natural. He doesn't seem like the type who spends a lot of time in front of the mirror. Though, to be fair, sometimes it takes a lot of work to look like you don't spend a lot of time in front of a mirror...). It reminds me of Mom's appreciation, and is interesting to me. I think it takes courage to acknowledge your funny parts and to let them amuse you, while also adding to your confidence.

***

Especially as a woman, I've heard and participated in many discussions on the dangers of comparison. I understand the concern, I do. If you walk around with Better Than Me Goggles on, you'll miss much joy and fulfillment. I understand the general tendency to size ourselves up next to so-and-so and immediately find the impressive features of the other person, only to then make ourselves feel better by finding their unimpressive features.

Comparing your blog to her blog. Your parties to her parties. Your dinners to her dinners. Your education to her education. Your haircut to her haircut. Your vocabulary to her vocabulary. Your social skills to her social skills. Your 'abs' to her abs. And so we often hear well-intentioned caution against this habit. "Don't look at others and compare yourself, just look to the Lord!" "Comparison at its core is discontentment!"

I'm going to toss a different ball at you. I think comparison, not in the "how I find my worth and validity" way, but in the "thoughtfully noting similarities and differences" way, can be incredibly beneficial to our hearts. Go ahead, notice how people are different — even better — than you are. It's okay. Be honest with yourself (not falsely humble, but honest). Discover the freedom of accepting and actually being grateful that other people have things you don't and are good at things you are not. Not only does it make this life more interesting, but it gives you the chance to develop more fully. You aren't stuck to being the person who is only able to do (or even appreciate) A, B and C. You get to dabble in K and learn more about R and perhaps even love X. My observation is that when it comes to female bodies, especially, there is far more variety to appreciate and love than we let ourselves believe.

I've been a photographer since 2007. As an artist professionally I can assure you that excellence and inspiration are some of the keys to my success. My mom took me to the Salvador Dali Art Museum in Florida and it weirded me out in a memorable way. He was a brilliant freak. His mind confuses me, and his talent is clear. I don't even particularly care for surrealist art, and yet I was intrigued by this colorful, kaleidoscope man and his paintings. They were (well, most of them) excellent. And so weird. A dear friend dragged me into the San Francisco MoMa, and I watched her bawl feelings out of her eyes over a large red painting. I went to the National Museum of Art a few days after my mom died and I looked at an airy, blended field of grass by Van Gogh and felt as though I had spent a moment inside the field myself. While visiting The National Gallery in Trafalgar Square, London, I looked upon Seurat, Vermeer, da Vinci, Monet and some of these masterpieces seemed "eh" compared to other lesser-known paintings in the building. I sit on my bed and scroll through pages of true talent displayed on social media. The excellent among them take my breath away and fly it to the moon. Inspiration.

The focus, the clarity, the dedication it took all of these artists to create what they offer to the world gives me a healthy dose of butt-kick and happiness. Gosh I'd like to make someone feel with my art the way she made me feel with her art. I don't want to copy her art. No, no. I want to make my own. Comparing, noting, enjoying, processing, praising a job-well-done is nourishment for my soul and stirring to my skill.

***

The Artist did a great job with His art, with you — not just "the inside you." Your body has been carefully and beautifully crafted. And I think it is right to appreciate what the Craftsman has done. I think it's right to appreciate His other bodies of work too. That feeling of wanting to hide was Adam and Eve's first instinct after the original sin. It wasn't God's heart for us to be ashamed of ourselves. It isn't His heart, still!

My mom was a constant voice, affirming my body throughout my whole life. I would stand in front of a mirror in tears and she'd walk me through the "I'm sorry, everyone feels this way sometimes" phase, to the "Look at you! You're beautiful!" phase, to the "You just need to change your mindset. It's time to stop." phase.

Alfre Woodard said, "Everybody has a part of her body that she doesn't like, but I've stopped complaining about mine because I don't want to critique nature's handiwork. My job is simply to allow the light to shine out of the masterpiece." It's funny how there are times in life when you just don't get it. You just don't appreciate something like being young until you're old. About being wide awake until you're tired. About being full until you're hungry.

I saw an interview with Tina Fey and Amy Poehler where they were answering questions fielded to them by young women. "What is one thing women in their 20's shouldn't worry about?" Without skipping a beat Tina said "Their bodies. Your body? It looks fantastic. Take a million pictures." I nodded in agreement, thinking of myself at 20 and how I felt insecure, obsessive, and never good enough. "All those young girls who don't even know what they have," I mentally tsk-tsk-ed. It wasn't until a few hours later, when the thought crossed my mind again, that I realized I still AM in my twenties! Married and three pregnancies into my twenties, but still young! I laughed out loud at myself. I guess I'm still learning. But I have taken her advice and snapped more pictures in my last pregnancy, and I'm even kind of looking forward to my fluffy pooch when this baby comes out. And I'm kind of looking forward to eventually overcoming some personal challenges in a balanced, guilt-free, grace-full way.

***

"How to talk to your daughter about her body, step one: Teach her how it works. Don't you dare talk about how much you hate your body in front of your daughter. Encourage your daughter to run because it makes her feel less stressed. Encourage your daughter to climb mountains because there is nowhere better to explore your spirituality than the peak of the universe. Encourage your daughter to surf, or rock climb, or mountain bike because it scares her and that's a good thing sometimes. Help your daughter love soccer or rowing or hockey because sports make her a better leader and a more confident woman. Explain that no matter how old you get, you'll never stop needing good teamwork. Never make her play a sport she isn't absolutely in love with. Teach your daughter how to cook kale. Teach your daughter how to bake chocolate cake made with six sticks of butter. Maybe you and your daughter both have thick thighs or wide ribcages. It's easy to hate these non-size zero body parts. Don't. Tell your daughter that with her legs she can run a marathon if she wants to, and her ribcage is nothing but a carrying case for strong lungs. She can

scream and she can sing. Remind your daughter that the best thing she can do
with her body is to use it to mobilize her beautiful soul."
–Sarah Koppelman

The sentences about kale and butter-cake got my attention. That was my mom. She taught me to make a rainbow with a meal. "Try to always have shades of red, green, and yellow on your plate." A bowl of chili, a slice of bread, a side of Caesar salad. Taco salad, corn on the cob, and watermelon. Glazed chicken, steamed broccoli, and a small glass bowl of strawberry yogurt. Mom was so balanced in nutrition and she made healthy, robust meals for us when she was in the kitchen. And yet she was the number one downer of chips and queso at our favorite Mexican restaurant, and she was notorious for fast food stops to share a "piping hot" sleeve of fries and a small milkshake. She would make herself a stash of sour cream dip to go with her crinkle-cut potato chips and favorite evening dramas. She loved eating healthy, light and fresh, and she loved eating buttery, cheesy and cheap.

In-between her babies she would try fad diet after fad diet to lose those pregnancy pounds, but they never lasted. And in her final years she really regretted not just enjoying the food she was able to eat. More than that, she regretted not deeply enjoying her healthy body more while she had it. She had always loved the sun, loved to be outside, loved the ocean and pool, loved walking all day in a theme park, loved giving birth. She had lived grateful for her body, but knowing that the end was near gave her especial perspective. She loved being able to use her body in whatever ways she could, with whatever time she had left.

In the weeks before her second cancer diagnosis she discovered she had lymphedema in her left arm. Lymphedema is excessive swelling in your arms or legs caused by blockage (and is very typical for cancer patients to experience after treatment, especially of the lymph nodes). Her one arm had tripled in size and made her quite the Michelin Lady! There is no cure for this condition, but it can be managed with therapy and compression sleeves (and Mama got herself a snuggly, quilted-pink one!). During her next rounds of treatments she experienced a great amount of burning in her swollen arm and the tightness combined with pain made it hard for her to move her fingers or lift her arm.

That's why I'll never forget her braiding hair. Her — thankfully somewhat naive — youngest daughters knew Mom was very sick; but somehow when you're a little girl, Mom is just Mom. And without hesitation or worry the girls with their thick, long hair would bounce into her room at night and ask if Mom could brush and braid their hair (so they wouldn't have tangles the next day). Mom never, ever declined. Sometimes my other sister and I, and even Caleb, would intercept them and do their hair before Mom was asked. But if they made it to her, she happily and slowly did what moms get to do — used her breaking body — soaking up the chance to do so. It hurt her fingers and her arm, but there was no way she was passing up the opportunity.

A few weeks before she died she asked if there was anything I wanted from her or that I wanted for us to try to do together. I'm not much of a crier but it was hard to get through this request. While Caleb and I were still dating, I had seen her save a DIY baby mobile idea to a online-board with the caption "I'm going to make this for my first granddaughter someday!" I hated to ask, but I also hated to never have it. She sent me off to find an old lamp shade, vintage floral sheets, and needle and thread. She propped herself up in bed and with one hand cut strips of fabric, wrapped the wire frame, pinned it into place, and even sewed a few stitches to secure it. I tried to help her but she really wanted to do it herself. "Your body is meant to be used up." (ND Wilson)

It might have taken close to five minutes, but she walked up the stairs by herself until the last days. She peeled herself from her bed, if it was in any way possible, and watched her children play sports from the minivan, because she was too tired to get to a seat on the sideline. The kids grew very fond of the cheering-horn from the back of the field!

"Generally, by the time you are Real, most of your hair has been loved off, and your eyes drop out and you get loose in the joints and very shabby." (Margery Williams) Her cozily-squishy belly was long gone and toddlers could no longer dive aggressively and playfully into her lap. She could fit both of her legs into one of those Myrtle Beach-days swimsuit holes. Her size 0 pants hung off her sadly and her size 14-16's all of a sudden seemed desirable. Wigs made other people feel more comfortable (and her too, in the right context), but mostly they were an itching, obvious nuisance. After giving birth to me and coming home to her bedroom mirror, she remembers standing in a bit of worried awe as she stared at herself. "This is my body? MY goodness…!" She went through a similar process of getting reacquainted with her new body many times in the following decades. Bald, burned, breast-less, steroid-stuffed, skeletal, flakey, intubated, leaking, and rashed.

I can't tell you the power it gave me to watch her, with such shabby beauty and willing elegance, embrace her life and body those last years, after knowing her during healthier times. A power to enjoy my body and to embrace the very great gift it is to move inside it. It's not about minimizing the body, either. Acting like the body is superficial or is a waste of time is flat wrong. It's living in the balance: mentally, emotionally, and physically healthy enough to make healthy choices, yet healthy enough to enjoy the "purely for pleasure" parts, not giving oneself over entirely to either side.

***

When I fly over the dirt streaks of Utah or the sand dunes in Arizona, I see Earth's stretch marks, where the ground has ripped, then flowed and held together. There are red canyons on the skin of earth. I know what it would feel like to run my fingers across the tops of the torn land. Both the midwest and my middle are beautiful, and not because they are flat and smooth. My belly looks like white, pocked, puffed bread dough now. And the feet that once plowed from the inside now plow from the outside, still smashing and kicking. He kneads me. He needs me. The rolls. "...and the bread that I will give is my flesh." (John 6:33) I tell him to hold still and stop wiggling but he presses into me hard. "Ow! STOP it!" We do communion with our bodies, we do communion in our breaking and crying, with the whine. "I'm serious!" He looks up at me with sorry-looking, beautiful eyes. I feel sorry for being snappy. We hold each other and find rest in the softest places of each other.

I look in the mirror and when I grab that stomach in my fist it looks like cinnamon rolls which is like Christmas which is like Giving which is "for unto us a Child is born." Yes, Body, for unto us a child was born. It started with blood before summer camp and before all the other girls I knew. It started with secret meetings in the bathroom with a small blue and green box and the vent fan on loud. 143 blood cycles later, there was another body inside mine. It feels a little bit "ew!" to write about, and it's not something I talk face to face with hardly anyone about. Maybe it's crude and inappropriate — but maybe it's something we all know about and maybe it's how we have actual life. Implantation spotting, vomiting blood into the toilet, blood draws at Quest Lab, bloody gums (floss more, mama), my blood-streaked warm baby laid upon me in the birth room, the enormous blood pads, the smaller blood pads, cracked nipples, our first anniversary after having a baby, a big fall when I tried to go running after giving birth, 144 cycles. "This is my blood, which is poured out for you. This is my body, given for you." (Luke 22)

I hope it's not unfitting to compare fussy nap time to the holy sacraments or having one baby to saving the entire world by conquering death. To compare myself, born in 1989, to YHWH, The Father of Lights. But we share with Him.

We share in His world, in His home, in His family, in His body, in His analogies. He shows us pictures and postcards and scars of what it's all about, while we wait patiently to see and feel the whole scene ourselves. We maybe don't know about groaning under the weight of heavenly wrath, but we know about groaning in L&D Room 304A. We maybe don't know how strong His love is for His children, but we know how strong our love is for our children. We maybe don't have scars on our side from a sword at the end of life, but we have scars on our sides to make new life. We maybe don't understand the close kindred bond of the Trinity or how safely-welcomed into that relationship we are, but we know what happens when we call to someone who answers us. We maybe don't understand how much more brightly we'll be able to see, but we know the difference when we put our contact lenses into our earthly eyes. We get to live in the metaphors and hints and these bodies.

"We know that the whole creation has been groaning as in the pains of childbirth right up to the present time. Not only so, but we ourselves, who have the first fruits of the Spirit, groan inwardly as we wait eagerly for our adoption to sonship, the redemption of our bodies. For in this hope we were saved. But hope that is seen is no hope at all. Who hopes for what they already have? But if we hope for what we do not yet have, we wait for it patiently."
–Romans 8:22

One more day, one more trip around the sun, one more moment in the Son, one more chance in this body. Do what you will with it, but do not be ashamed of it. Use it. Even if it jiggles or cracks or has to lay down a lot. Use it as well as you are able, knowing there will be seasons of "more" and "less" able. Knowing that is okay. Knowing you're alive.

What Mama Bear Taught Me About...
5. MESSES

"This is the shame of being ashamed, the lassitude that makes junk accumulate, the shame that tells you there is another way to live but you are too dumb to find it." — Brene Brown

My mother was known for her laid-back nature. Of course when I was young I didn't realize what people meant by that because she was just "Mom" to me, but I remember hearing it often. "Your mom is so relaxed! I wish I was more like her!" "She's so chill and go-with-the-flow." "I feel like your mom is never stressed!" She let us play outside with shoes off and play inside with shoes on. Her reasoning? "It'll make your feet tougher. If you want to wear shoes you'll put them on yourself. I don't need to reinforce another rule. Floors are floors, and any germs you trek in will build your immune system."

But she was not orderly — in mind or deed. While she had excellent taste in design, and could plan a Christmas Party worthy of the cover page of *Southern Living*, the upstairs and every hall closet was stuffed with clutter and boxes and hidden junk. Piles of papers filled her desk, decorated her nightstand, and lined the walkways of the house. Our car was a scattered monument to big soccer wins, urgent french-fry runs, and the assembled wardrobes of a flock of children. She would begin one project then abandon it half-way through. She would get into the middle of a past chore, run out to carpool, make a meal (and wreck in the kitchen), pay a bill, and move the loads of laundry that had been started three days before — before hunkering in for a night of reality TV and piles of mail to sort. Once we found a small sunflower plant growing in the folds of damp clothes in the washing machine — a seed must have been in someone's pocket. It had enough time and enough moisture to sprout. Wups.

She was a mix of over-ambition, lofty vision, laziness, and serenity; blended with in-born personality, creativity, and physiological hoarder-tendencies. It was the area of her life where she felt like the biggest failure, but in the failing she certainly had tried. I can't count the number of times she implemented a new chore-chart system, created morning-routines for us, or spent days getting one whole part of the house in perfect order. She would routinely instruct us all to bring in as much as we could from the car or to empty the dishwasher so she could fill it. We'd set timers and all be given a room to put back together. Knowing how important it was to my dad, she'd often have us stop our playing and our homework and get the first floor tidy so he could come home from work to a clean house. They hired maids and professional organizers, and my dad did more housework in a year than most men we know do in their whole lives.

It just wasn't in her nature. Beautiful spaces were in her nature. Welcoming people in and nurturing them were in her nature. Enjoying, well, anything was in her nature. But keeping up a house? It wasn't there.

***

My dad once made an observation to me that every person's character strength is of the same nature as their character weakness. He was saying that usually you don't have to change entire qualities, you just have to put your qualities to work in the right places. I've thought on that idea much. I think it's true. Someone's determination is also their stubbornness. Someone's kindness and patience is also their passive indifference. Someone's ability to talk well and long is also their tendency to talk too much. A personal hunger and drive can be their inability to stop and remember what is important. And as far as my mom was concerned, her laid-back ways were also her un-industriousness.

Laying aside the potential problems that might be found in a messy person, I learned from my mom the corresponding character strengths and the God-like qualities of being messy. God is not overwhelmed by mess, in fact, it's even a place He can shine. "Life isn't like a book. Life isn't logical or sensible or orderly. Life is a mess most of the time. And theology must be lived out in the midst of that mess." (Charles Colson) He is comfortable in miry bogs, stables of manure, and earth itself — which is great news for us. And particularly encouraging, I believe, for people like me: people who are messy.

In a group of women I polled, nearly all of them reported a sense of shame or embarrassment about their messy places being seen. Here are several sample confessions:

"Yes, yes, and yes. Embarrassed, all the time. My trunk is full of stuff from the times I've remembered that someone else is going to be in my car and I needed to get rid of the cups and the old tupperware containers that I keep forgetting to take out."

"I totally feel embarrassed. When people ask me to drive and I haven't had the time to throw out the fast food, garbage, water bottles etc,. I literally will make up an excuse for them to drive because its so embarrassing to reveal how I keep my vehicle looking!"

"I ALWAYS feel embarrassed when people see my car or house without me being able to clean it. I avoid giving people rides as much as I possibly can. When it

comes to hosting, though, I don't avoid it, I just get really stressed out and yell at my husband to help me clean before they come over."

"It's so disappointing to watch your hard work of cleaning, after mustering up the courage, only to have it unravel shortly afterwards. I do feel overwhelmed."

"I think the main reason I just cannot make myself clean is because it feels so useless. I don't understand how people can keep it together all the time and often wish I could just have someone do all my cleaning for me."

I am grateful for their honest answers. I hope to encourage those who share the sentiments of the women above, as well as uplift any who are orderly and don't "get" people who are different. We were not made to live in shame and embarrassment, and God is indeed found throughout all creation.

***

This topic goes back to the very beginning. A new couple, living in their outdoor space, assigned to keep it, to care for it, to order it, to enjoy it. The human race, according to scripture, was formed by God taking flecks of dust and turning them into a person. That stuff that layers our shelves, that settles on our side tables, that hides in the corners of our picture frames, is — we are told — the stuff from which we are all made. After Adam and Eve first dirtied themselves, they covered themselves. They hid, then lied. They ruined the dream home given to them, where working wasn't a chore and enjoyment was their job. They were banished to the hard ground, to hard toil, to hard dirt.

The entire Old Testament is, in effect, many stories of the people who came from Adam and Eve trying to be and stay clean. Paragraph after paragraph of tedious delineation between what is "clean and unclean, holy and common." "Do not let your hair become unkempt and do not tear your clothes, or you will die and the Lord will be angry with the whole community. This is a lasting ordinance for the generations to come, so that you can distinguish between the holy and the common, between the unclean and the clean, and so you can teach the Israelites all the decrees the Lord has given them through Moses." (Leviticus 10:6)

The command from heaven was that cleanliness is godliness. The wrong kind of animal, prepared the wrong way, eaten in the wrong setting, was a death sentence. Sickness and disease weren't just a physical hurdle, it was rejection of you as a person. Cleansing, purifying, and washing weren't just for the one who was "high-maintenance," it was for anyone who wanted God's approval and access to His presence. The standards were, purposefully, impossibly high and were centered around becoming clean.

When Jesus and His placenta tore vaginal tissue and He lay naked on His sweating mother's bare chest, while she settled on hay surrounded by flies and barnyard smells — He changed everything. When He touched bleeding women, grubby toddlers, terminally-sick men, and corpses — He was doing more than healing and welcoming. He was making bold announcements about the heart of Heaven, about the King Himself. You don't have to come all cleaned up, anymore. You may come as you are. I love you, even dirty. I'm here with you, I can handle this mess. Don't fix yourself up and approach me only after you've gotten it all together. Martha, you're busy serving, you're busy cleaning, you're busy trying to impress me. Come be with me. Prodigal son, covered in pig slop: let me hold you close and dress you in my finest. Don't worry if your shoes track in some mud. Just come in!

***

The "spirit of welcome" with which Jesus both visited earth and invited all to an eternal home is the welcoming-gift that He also implanted in my mother. When she was a baby her parents relocated from Orange County, California to a smaller, dustier city in Nevada. Her dad had been offered a new job at a bank; and it was certainly more affordable to live across state lines, while still having the perks of being close to the regional highlights they loved. My grandmother was supportive of the move but was horrified to be buying a brand new house, in an idyllic neighborhood, for $32,000. The number seemed outrageous to her, and she felt a bit guilty for spending so much on something for herself. She vowed then and there that her home would be her offering to the Lord and that she would use it to love and serve God and others in any way she could.

My mom grew up in a home with a revolving door of guests, potluck dinners, single mothers with chubby babies, friends of friends needing a place to crash, bunko nights, and an open-house policy. She carried that heart with her into adulthood and eventually into marriage and mothering. My parents both demonstrated and taught us an eager, excited generosity of self. Time, home, space, energy, money, rides — they made themselves available to the people in their lives. If someone happened to stop in while a meal was being prepared they insisted that the passer-by stay and eat, and were nearly offended, if they didn't. During sports seasons it was most normal to have someone's teammate sleeping over or staying the weekend. A variety of times they had couples living in the basement (though they functioned more like a part of the household). They were legal guardians to a young basketball player who needed some stability. They didn't necessarily have the time, or money, or space, at least by normal cultural perception, but they knew in reality they did. They knew that no matter how tight finances were or how packed the house was, they had been given much and they were happy to share whatever it was they had. It was messy and it was extra work, but their home—and their lives—were open.

***

In modern, first-world culture I notice that messiness is frowned upon (or at least needs a defender). We apologize for "the mess" when someone stops in. We write her off as being "a hot mess." My earlier-referenced poll was of a group of women who claimed they are naturally-messy, and it was fascinating how nearly every one of them admitted that they don't like to have people over if their house is messy. There is an embarrassment and shame that comes with someone else seeing your mess. It would be simply inaccurate to conclude that there are "clean people" and "messy people." The subject is large — and certainly complex. There are spiritual messes, emotional messes, physical messes, relational messes, mental messes.

God tends to use analogy (like comparing the grey gloominess of rainy weather to the forlorn experience of crying and being sad of heart). I'm convinced that our physical messes aid in understanding the tangles, clutter, and weariness of heart. There is something important, something from God, when admitting "I don't have this place in order, but I still want you here. Can you come as I am?"

There is nothing quite as hopeful and helpful to my heart as friends who know me well, come into my world as it is, and enjoy me without comments, facial expressions, or disgusted body language. They don't have to pretend they are someone they are not — and neither do I. This creates fertilizer to soul soil where such lovely blossoms grow.

"Where there are no oxen, the manger is clean, but abundant crops come by the strength of the ox" (Proverbs 14:4). Derek Kidner says that, "Orderliness can reach the point of sterility. This proverb is [a plea for] the readiness to accept upheaval, and a mess to clear up, as the price of growth." Cleanliness isn't necessarily sterility, but messiness isn't necessarily disgusting. While some might need more motivation to "get up and do it!" others might need the encouragement to sit down and rest. Regardless, if "both types" want to love and want to give what they can offer, the best things will happen.

"Mrs. Joe was a very clean housekeeper, but had an exquisite art of making her cleanliness more uncomfortable and unacceptable than dirt itself."
–Charles Dickens

More than clean, and more than messy, what is important is available. Willing. I am willing to be inconvenienced. I am willing to be an inconvenience. I am willing to work hard, yet I am willing to stop working. I am willing to let you come into this vulnerable place and see the mess. I am willing to let you come into this ordered place and undo it. I am willing to listen and not just fix the issues I see. I am willing to help and walk alongside you as you try to change. I am here, I am focused, and you are more than welcome — cluttered counters or smudged-bathroom-mirrors or to-do lists, aside.

***

"Scruffy hospitality means you're not waiting for everything in your house to be in order before you host and serve friends in your home. Scruffy hospitality means you hunger more for good connection and serving what you have, not what you don't have. Scruffy hospitality means you're more interested in quality conversation than the impression your home or lawn makes. If we only share meals with friends when we're excellent, we aren't truly sharing life together. Don't allow a to-do list to disqualify you from time with people you're called to love in friendship. We tell our guests 'come as you are,' perhaps we should tell ourselves 'host as you are.' Hospitality is not a house inspection, it's friendship."
–Jack King

Since I was raised by parents who naturally bent differently on this issue, I feel fortunate to have a well-rounded view. My mom's heart was: I want to make people more important than my house or things. My dad's heart was: taking care of our house and things is loving people and making them important. They were both right. It's not fair to say "God doesn't care about your house being clean, He only cares that you are loving others!" because people who work hard to keep their houses in order are often doing so to love the people who come and do life in their homes. It's right to respect and appreciate their effort and love. It's also not fair to believe that an undone house is a lack of love or character. In many instances, it's the very opposite. God does care about our things and our houses, but I think He most cares about why. Why do we let people into the walls? Why do we take such good or poor care of our things? Can we sit in the mess? Can we learn to restore order? Can we see, and even enjoy, God in both?

In the late months of 2015, as I'm writing this, minimalism and simplicity are all the rage. A book released last year was eaten up by readers with instruction on ridding your life of clutter. Capsule wardrobes have hit the scene; and the pinnacle of much current design is empty, white space. But I like a lot of the suggestions and reasons for these trends. Much of it is very helpful for a junk-accumulator like me. This vision isn't — can't be! — everything. Have you ever seen pictures of Positano on the Amalfi Coast? The staggered, vibrantly colored buildings are crammed (dare I say cluttered) onto a steep, disorganized mountainside. Minimalism would ruin every bit of magic in such a wonderfully hectic view.

My mom's best friend has taken us to her family's lake house in a secluded, mountain town in Pennsylvania. It's a nook-and-cranny house, with mismatched furniture, stuffed bookshelves, eclectic decor hanging on almost all the walls, creaks in the floors, and tiny rooms leading to more tiny rooms. It would be a shame to knock down walls and create a modern, open floor plan or take down all the "eyesores" for a simpler dusting routine. There is imagination and tradition in the cramped quarters. The classic outdoor markets in Marrakech, Kyoto, and Brasilia are a madness and a comfort all their own. The yelling, the crowds, the subconscious sounds of large bells, the energy, the being pushed, the smells, the wares, the rumble. It's no hushed stroll through a topiary garden in Mount Vernon. But it's good. They are both good.

I imagine the art rooms in heaven splattered with paint, the history of colors on palettes and aprons. The bakeries must be puffed with flour, and used spoons certainly will be left to lick. The One who lives there is the One who thought that leaves falling into messy piles on the floor was a grand idea. He's the one who came up not only with child-birth, but with four-days-after-child-birth. He looks happily on scenes of wet mothers and wet babies in the shadows on unmade beds. Leaking breasts, soggy diapers, bloody pads, milk drips across cheeks, tears maybe, too.

He dumps snow on the rug with the playful abandon of my son emptying a jar of glitter. He allowed dandelions to leave their crumbs anywhere they please (and they're magic crumbs, because they grow more fluffy puffs when they land). It's nearly impossible to tell the difference between a pile of sawdust left by a busy carpenter bee or a busy carpenter husband. Left to grow on their own, thickets and fields are a beautiful, unsymmetrical, wild, productive wreck. The best sex leaves sheets and comforters and pillows out of place, and twisted into a happy spread. There is nothing quite like a big sports win on a bad weather day: the mix of mud, grass, sweat, untucked shirts, stringy hair and Gatorade are stunning accessories to a celebrating athlete. Shucking corn is a worthwhile mess to make. Have you ever seen a small child happily picking and eating strawberries or finishing off a few slices of watermelon? The red juice was our Maker's idea. I don't think He's worried about the stains.

Naturally messy people can be a declaration of God's unlimited welcome and they can encourage the blessing of "coming as you are." No rushing around, no hiding in boxes, no peaking out from behind a closed door. I believe there is abundant freedom in relating to Him, and others, with a deep-sighing breath of relief. I would love to see a world, particularly for women, where having "the perfect body, the perfect home" aren't the first things we notice or attack about each other. I'd love for us to be more well-rounded thinkers and to have a more nuanced understanding — for ourselves and for others — about what 'mess" is and about what "clean" is. I'd love for passengers in cars to be first (and mostly) grateful that someone is taking the time to move them from Point A to Point B — no matter the state of the vehicle. I'd love to not feel those inner-belly pangs when someone shows up and sees Unprepared Me. One of my favorite answers in my earlier mentioned survey expressed exactly what I hoped to communicate by writing this chapter:

"I don't want my lifestyle to be anti-hospitable. I want my husband to be able to bring people home and know that I won't freak out. I see my home as a tool, not as a full time job. I'd like to keep it running 'smoothly' so it doesn't get in the way of ministry or the work we're trying to get done; but I never want it to own me. I prefer transparency over a fake magazine life. I feel like I can offer people what I have — whether the home or car is clean or not. It's available. Honestly, in my mind, everything is temporary. The house is a wreck? No worries, it'll be clean if I take the time out to do it. Does it actually look spotless and beautiful? Well, I know that won't last! But, I'll enjoy it while I can! Everything in this world is changing constantly. Left to itself, it will decay. With time and work, it can be improved. That's just how the world works. The thing I struggle with is how to prioritize my time. I see people and relationships as much more important, and these treasures take precedence over my idea of a spotless home."

***

My mom made our home and her life an invitation — a "yes." Floors were scratched, rugs were stained, dishes were broken, blankets were ripped, books were torn, lamps were smashed, piles were piled, couches were bounced on, laundry usually sat and sat and sat. She happily used up her resources. Not much of anything was left in "brand new condition." She didn't rage when crayons melted in cushions or ketchup blotted seats in the car. She never seemed bothered when I wanted to help in the kitchen — her peaceful, calm demeanor made me feel confident, special, and like she wanted me there. I wasn't a nuisance with my six measuring cups. It was easy for her to set aside a to-do (or should-do) list and give me her undivided attention. And when she really couldn't stop everything, she let me chatter away while she multi-tasked; and she'd chatter right back. She lived like everything else was the nuisance and I was what mattered most.

"As Jesus and his disciples were on their way, he came to a village where a woman named Martha opened her home to him. She had a sister called Mary, who sat at the Lord's feet listening to what he said. But Martha was distracted by all the preparations that had to be made, distracted by serving. She came to him and asked, 'Lord, don't you care that my sister has left me to do the work by myself? Tell her to help me!' 'Martha, Martha,' the Lord answered, 'you are worried and upset about many things, but few things are needed—or indeed only one. Mary has chosen what is better, and it will not be taken away from her.'"
–Luke 10:38-42

What Mama Bear Taught Me About...
6. FLEXIBILITY

"The measure of intelligence is the ability to change." — Albert Einstein

For a few years now I've been in the "Yup, Mom was right" phase of life. I presume this will continue until I'm gone. "Make sure your nails are at least clean before doing anything professional." "If you feel bad about yourself, go for a hard run." "Grammar matters." Of course, one of her pieces of advice was, "Someday you're going to realize that I was right!" "Be flexible," Mom would say. "You have to be flexible! I will not raise you to be a rigid person!"

It was very important to my mom that I wasn't someone who fell apart unnecessarily easily. "Don't be rigid...or else you'll break," she'd say, "I'm not going to raise rigid children!" She chose to battle for well-rounded, balanced, flexible in her mothering. One dictionary definition of flexible says: "Capable of bending easily without breaking, able to be easily modified, and ready to respond to altered circumstances or conditions."

As I'm writing about this, I realize that I never specifically asked her why or where she got this determination to raise versatile little people. I wish I had. If I had to guess, however, I think it would come from her own difficulties through the many parts of her life and from how many things did "not go as she expected." My understanding is that it was exacting and painful for her to realize her plans were not going to unfold as she hoped. I know she struggled with being bitter or begrudged. I think she also had such positive experiences in the "unplanned" or "change of plans" that she had a deep soul gratitude and respect for the surprises in life.

From what I know of her — and I knew her pretty well — I believe she wanted us to have as little struggle and as much fun and hope in God's plan as possible, during our inevitable experiences of the "C word": change. She never imagined she would join the army. She never imagined she would live, long term, away from California — all the way on the other side of the country outside Washington DC. She never imagined she would not get married until her 30's. She never imagined she would have seven kids. She never thought she would lose her mom suddenly, without getting to say goodbye. She never thought she was going to miss most of the "big life milestones" for most of her kids. She really did think she was going to get to those scrapbooks someday. But she was forced to bend when conditions changed, and she did so beautifully.

***

The woman had a good head on her shoulders and was keen to the lessons of life. She really loved being a mother, and (this is different) she really loved each of us. She told me once that she never felt resentful of us or like we had held her back from something else she could have done with her life. I told her that I had read and heard from a number of women who have struggled with those feelings (and the guilt that comes with them) and I asked her why she thinks she had the positive experience she did. (God knows it wasn't because we were such a charm-bracelet-family to raise!) "Well, mostly," she said, "because my mom loved being a mom and I wanted to be just like her. She made my life so wonderful and seemed so happy with us. I wanted to be that to someone else."

Her opinion was also that getting married "later than planned" helped her get some of those curiosities out of her system. People didn't talk about "finding your passion" the way they do now; but her work as a nurse was extremely fulfilling to her intellectually, emotionally, and spiritually. Science and biology were her favorite subjects, and she loved to take care of people. It was the perfect fit and very much a match to her deepest heart passions and interests. She also moved! Away from home! She told me about leaving her hometown, where she finished college and had her first nursing job, to leave for boot camp and training in Texas. "This was all pre-internet you know!! I had to figure this out with phone calls and letters in the mail!" The many question-marks filling the page of her life in that season started to make her feel panicky. She recalled to me that she told herself "One step at a time, Sue. You have a plane ticket. You have an address. So you will get on a plane. That's the first step. Once you are there, you can figure out how to get to the next place. But you don't have to worry about that now. There will be a cab or a shuttle or a ride. It's Texas not Antarctica. You'll be able to figure it out."

I was surprised to hear her say this because the woman I knew was so not a panicky or nervous person! She had absorbed the lessons very well, I suppose, because her anthem was "We'll figure it out!" It's neat to me that she spent a whole decade of adult life (very formative adult life!) all by herself. I know there were the loneliest hours and pangs of envy and fear of "What if a family of my own isn't in the cards for me?" But in the meantime she was becoming such a capable, courageous, smart, flexible woman. I don't feel like she "grew up with us" like wives and mothers (like myself!) who marry or give birth young might experience. She grew up before us. My dad married a competent, life-built woman — not a little girl. Likewise, she was not "a baby having a baby," rather she was grown and elegant in herself. Those alone years, those travels, those missions trips, those roommates, those degrees, those new jobs, those changes of plans were good for her. I realized after she died that she spent more of her life unmarried and *nulligravida* than she did as a wife and mother. What a concept!

***

On my 16th birthday my parents came into my bedroom at 5:14 in the morning and whisper-sang "Happy Birthday" to me. "Get your shoes on! Follow us!" I could see Mom's thrill even though the room was almost fully dark. The three of us got in the car and I had no idea where we were going. The only thing that came to mind briefly was "Maybe a new car...?" But my parents were not car-on-your-16th-birthday people, and I couldn't fathom that they would actually do that with me, knowing they have six other kids coming along. That's a high bar to set! And they didn't.

We pulled up to Einstein Bagels a few miles from our home. Toasted onion bagels with melted butter were my childhood favorite breakfast so they were treating me. We got there too early as it didn't open until 6:00 am. We three sat in the parking lot half-asleep. "Isn't this special?" Mom chuckled from the front seat. We walked into the shop with the probably 17-year-old clerk, who struggled with the keys. He flipped on the lights in the cafe area, started up the cash register, and caught up with the staff in the kitchen. We sat down at a table but had to get the chairs down from stacks in the corner ourselves. It was still completely black outside as we ate, and Mom pulled out a bag from her purse. Dad took over. "So, you can open this and then I'll explain it." I pulled out a beautiful halo cut ring with my birth stone from a real jewelry store. "Okay," Dad continued, "this is not a promise ring." Mom tilted her head to the side and looked at me with a face like "Don't worry about it." But Dad went on: "This is just a ring that we are giving you because we love you." Mom spoke now "Yes. We love you very, very much and we hope you feel it!"

Purity or "save yourself sexually until marriage rings" were popular when I was a teenager. "If you want to make a promise like that, that's between you and God, not me and you." "We're not saying we think you should have sex!" Mom chimed in. I wore my beautiful ring and did indeed feel very special and loved. It wasn't until after I was married that I could appreciate how well my parents handled that exchange. My body and heart were not my dad's, or my mom's, they were mine. Their job was to love my mind, my body, my strength, and my soul. Their job was to provide for, train, support, teach, and nurture my mind, my body, my strength, and my soul. But ultimately they gave me a great sense of independence and self-responsibility — things I actually didn't even want!

***

I was newly dating a guy the year I turned 20 and neither of my parents were fond of him. I listened to their concerns and asked, "Well, what should I do? Tell me what to do." They said "We're not going to do that. You need to be able to take counsel, seek God, and make decisions yourself. It will not serve you as a woman to just do what you are told." I liked being told what to do. I liked the rules. They were clear. They were usually attainable. They gave me a scale by which I could chart myself. They were great.

"They give you a safety net so you don't have to take full responsibility for your actions, is what they do," Dad would insist. Mom wanted me to feel like I had thoroughly lived my life. She wanted me to be able to wrap myself around each stage and love it for what it actually was (not what someone else said it should be). Mom was right. Dad was right.

For most of our life as a family we were tethered to a cultural-center: our church community. This community was also our school community, our friend community, our art and sports community, and often even our neighborhood community. I want to be very, very clear: I am not writing about that church right now. There are valid, important (and personal) testimonies, opinions, and facts that I could share about that church; but that is a whole different topic. I don't mind discussing it. I just happen not to be discussing it right now. So when I share beliefs or practices or perspectives about God in the following paragraphs, I'm taking the responsibility upon myself and I'm sharing about my own heart.

The one thing I will say is that some of the greatest, most special memories of my life, to this day, happened inside that community. I, and my whole family, were the recipients of constant, flood-like, spiritual, physical, and emotional care for years and years. That community, at it's best, was truly God's hand moving upon the earth, holding His dear ones close and speaking through their actions, "I love you." I'm very very grateful. The topics of error, hurt, leadership, teaching style, authority, and whatever else was a part of that environment are real and they matter, but they are not the subject matter of this discussion. *End Caveat*

As I mentioned above, I was Rule Girl. I made it through all of Christian childhood believing there were two ways to live: of God or of the world. Not until my early twenties did I "discover" the third option the Bible presents: of your self. The self-righteous, "older brother," extremely polished and upright, A+, Bible-using, church-raised, obedient way to live — that isn't actually of the Lord or in His grace. Faith, worldliness, and legalism. Those are the categories. I misunderstood legalism because I only applied it to the justification part of my salvation. I had been (truly) well-trained and understood that being made new in Christ had two parts: being justified ("where justice is served, and you are found not guilty") and being sanctified (the process of becoming mature that happens between accepting Christ and death). I knew there was nothing I could add to my justification. I knew well that Jesus was not guilty and yet was treated as if He was. I knew I got to take

His perfection and claim it as mine because He was punished in my place and then gave me all of Himself. I knew no works, or "goodness," or even rule-keeping could add to the ultimate sacrifice He made. It was true: it was finished. I believed that. However, sanctification was where I could really shine. Sanctification was, of course, fueled by God but it was "my part" of the deal.

The Lord gave me the strength to be as good as I was, praise Him!, but it was me who was, you know, being really impressive. It was spiritual rigidity, and a big fat trap. My dad understood the bendable, flexible, far-reaching strength of grace in a way I didn't because of his "ugly" past. My mom was a "good church girl" like I was, but she was much more balanced and discerning. She had life under her belt and had seen enough of the wide world to be far more astute and gracious than I was. I was self-righteous, and they told me so. As they even grew in their own faith and understanding through my adult years, they continued to challenge me and be very open.

There were parts of their parenting they looked back on and said they would do differently. (I don't know how you can walk through such a journey as raising a human being and not have something you'd change.) Keeping the rules, keeping the plan, checking the list: made me look, and feel, really good. I could muscle myself to do almost anything if it would make me appear, or in my mind be, better. I didn't think through it that bluntly. I had myself fooled into believing I was "a thing" and was worthy of the high regards and remarks bestowed on me. But "To Him be the glory!" I'd croon.

"Since you died with Christ why do you submit to another set of rules: 'Do not handle! Do not taste! Do not touch!'? These rules, which have to do with things that are made to perish, are based on merely human commands and teachings. Such rigid regulations indeed have an appearance of wisdom, with their self-imposed worship, their false humility and their harsh treatment of the body, but they lack any value in restraining the indulgences of the heart." Colossians chapter 2 changed my life.

I had submitted myself to the outwardly spectacular, squeaky clean, highly impressive, rigid rules made by humans, including myself. I was embarrassed of the people in my family who had the gall to taint our family image. I was embarrassed by my parents when they made decisions for our family that went against what the respected people in our church community believed. I didn't feel love or interest for people who made different choices for their lives (in either direction) than I did. I felt defensive and eager to prove myself right. I was excessively aware of the opinions and standards of the people around us, and I was obsessed with being at the top and afraid of losing approval. It's strange to look back now and see, because I had no idea I was like that.

There was safety in numbers, safety in strictness. I knew what was expected of me, and I knew what to expect. It was like a job: train me for my role, tell me exactly what to do, and I'll show up, clock my hours, and do it. I played to the consciences of others and was terrified of being the "black sheep" who did something different. "For why is my freedom being judged by another's conscience? If I can take part in the meal with thankfulness, why am I denounced because of something I thank God for?" (1 Corinthians 10:29)

The revelation that saved my life was the flexible, fun, fascinating freedom available and desired for me. Once these puzzle pieces start to click together, I had a new view of everything, including my parents — especially Mom. God... liked me. God enjoyed my personality. God wanted me to have fun. God would indeed give me strength to grow. Yes, I would need to make actual, active decisions to participate in my life; but the point wasn't about getting it right and staying on my perceived version of the "perfect course." It was about living — really living! — and watching God bring about the growth in ways I could never have imagined. It felt like taking my little cart off the roller-coaster track and being put on the road for the first time. "You mean I can drive anywhere I want?" "Yup. Stay on the road. But go anywhere you want!"

Funny enough, the trust it takes to really live in freedom is far greater than what it takes to go around-and-around a dumb performance-loop. "What if I get lost?" "Do not be afraid." "But, seriously, what if I'm trying to get to the beach and I go the wrong way and I make a big mistake?" "Maybe you needed to see the mountains. Be flexible. Hush. Stop over thinking it. Have fun! Drive! Enjoy! Don't speed, stay on the road, and goooooo."

***

Not to belittle my mom's aptitude, but I firmly believe that her determination to help us be flexible was Holy Spirit-backed because God knew what was coming for our family. It wasn't going to be a controllable, standard life. We were going to need to be able to bend without snapping. We were going to need to adjust to a series of revisions to the plan. We were going to need to know that change in our life was not a change in God. To be "prepared to be surprised." It doesn't make the confusion, sadness, or struggle less real or even easier; but it has certainly grounded me through hard years in a way for which I just can't thank my mom enough.

For some people, life is as simple as a good routine and discipline. Things just kind of work out how they want them to, at least generally. But I believe for most people there is that shocking plot twist (or twists) they never saw coming, or at least hoped would never come. Flexibility, to me, is the posture of hands open, palms up. Rigidity, to me, is hands out, fists clenched. Fear or despondency, to me, is hands in my pockets, hidden away. As if saying "I don't want anything to do with this." To stand open and willing is hard. It means you're accepting, not controlling, what comes your way— for better or for worse — and that you're not going to clutch it when it's time for it to go. You will let the Master give and take and do His work, while you receive courage and love with abandon. It means you must have strong forearms and able shoulders but it also means you must be gentle and delicate when what is given is fragile. Then again, it means there will be seasons where you can't hold up those weary limbs any longer, so you rest them on the altar the Lord has slid beneath you. And you thank Him for His help, for His support, and you do not feel guilty. He has made Himself to be available, compassionately caring, and unfazed by plot-twists. By resting in Him you will have the ability you need to rise up again in the future, more capable than before.

***

Prepping to write this chapter I read an article that described "stubbornness" and "self-importance" as the opposite of "flexibility." I'm not sure if there is a better summation of my life in legalism: stubborn self-importance. I was very sure of my rules, and I was very significant thanks to my handling of them. *back of hand on forehead* "Oh wretch that I am!" "Flexibility will allow us to see our delight in the Lord, not in our plans or schedules." (Or, may I add, "abilities.") I sit here trying to knit together on paper what connects so well in my head.

I pause and close my eyes, longing to gather up thoughts. All that comes to mind is my mom, looking like she did when she was young. Thick, coarse, long hair. Her arms are full of children — they are hanging off her back and clinging to the fabric of her skirt. She's leading us onward as the sun sets and the long-shadowed, purplish-orange light traces her outline against the sky. She traverses the howling terrain of a rugged life, with mud on the hem of her flowing silk dress, pins falling out of her hair, sweat falling down her legs like rain drops on a glass window. She is saddled up, she carries us. Doggedly altruistic. Times come where she takes a deep breath and says "Ugh. I've been going the wrong direction. Okay. Let's turn around and continue on the way."

She was tough, but she was humble. With sadness in her eyes, she was very honest with me about flaws she had discovered in herself; that had not been in keeping with the heart of God. And she soldiered on. She took the brunt of our accusations, our confusion, our fears and let them break her heart. The stupid things that arrogant children say to get their way. The "dawning revelations" suddenly-deep teenagers have that are literally what they've been taught for their whole lives. The pointing fingers. "You and Dad didn't _____ enough." "You and Dad did _____ too much." She took it all. She was not rigid. I've referenced *The Velveteen Rabbit* many times since Mom has died: "Becoming Real takes a long time. That's why it doesn't happen often to people who break easily, or have sharp edges, or who have to be carefully kept."

What I saw in her was the triumphant, wooden sturdiness of the strength in freedom. She didn't need to defend herself, and she didn't need to obsessively control. She could float upon the water and welcome its course. She could stare death in the face and not even need to speak, "I am not afraid," because she wasn't and it showed. She didn't need to take it out on us. She was human. She had moments. She'd yell or cry or hide under the covers like human beings do. But she was marked by bending under the weight and not cracking. She was marked by believing beyond herself and re-navigating. She was marked by her all-time favorite verse — that real life is lived by trusting the Lord with all her heart, and not leaning on what she could understand. She was shaped by giving all her ways to Him, and being convinced He would make her path straight (Proverbs 3:5-6).

"I cannot see around this bend, or over this hill, but I will walk onward. He will straighten my course." Absolutely convinced of it. Especially in her final years, I saw her soften on long held practices that she realized were maybe just "good ideas for some" and not "Bible law" like she had once thought. I witnessed her come to terms with the end. "I never would have wished this for my life. I never would have wished this for my children. But I know God knows what He is doing. I believe it with my whole heart. One step at a time." she'd tell me — nourishing hope. Pliable like soft clay in the Potter's hands, willing to be whomever He wanted her to be, and willing to hold whatever she was made to hold. For her, that meant being single for longer than she would ever chosen. Then later it meant the love and anger and bodies of seven children. It meant a husband in a hard — but committed — marriage where they became true life partners. It meant being very sick and saying goodbye and leaving us all behind.

***

Since I was 13, I knew I wanted to have a career in the wedding industry. Not all little girls are little girls who daydream about their wedding day — but I was. In middle school, friends gave me subscriptions to bridal magazines as birthday gifts and my reward for finishing math homework was being allowed to go to theknot.com. My love of wedding-dreaming turned into an idea to be a wedding coordinator when I "grew up" and that plan quickly developed into becoming a wedding photographer instead. I was 14 when I second-shot my first wedding and 17 when I booked my own wedding clients. I watched the bridal gown shows, Bachelor reality-show weddings, the TLC wedding-competition shows, and the glamorous seven-figure celebrity specials. Before Pinterest I created my own "pin boards" with .jpeg files I'd find on the internet and save them in categorized folders. Flowers. Dresses. Hair-dos. Reception ideas.

My mom bought me a white lace, standing file cabinet to organize all the pages I tore out of magazines. She looked through them with me and never made fun when I changed my "definite" wedding color palette every few months. She'd let me pick her brain about all her wedding choices and which ones she'd do again and which ones she'd change.

She'd let me spout on and on about my dreeeaamm to rent a big house or two on a lake or at the beach or on a plantation. I wanted all the family, bridal party, and close friends to stay together and spend together the days leading up to the wedding. I wanted us setting-up together, staying up late together, working together, lingering together. I wanted lots of things, actually. But my young girl vision was of this packed-house, everyone-near, sharing a magical weekend isolated from the world with twinkle lights, lots of food, and bocce ball tournaments run by Dad.

Ten years later, Mom and I were 'finally' getting to plan my real wedding. She took me to Home Depot to get paint color chips so she could know exactly what my color palette was going to be ("I'm visual," she would remind). She had a huge board or two on Pinterest, full of ideas that she had stayed up way too late gathering. We found a perfect sized bed-and-breakfast in a Virginia vineyard. My dad called and they were going to make my long-held vision work within our budget. But Mom was dying.

This isn't what we planned. Her disease was so much worse this time. Her chemotherapy was about as intense as the doctors were willing to make it. She was in true physical suffering as her deflated, cancer-freckled lungs couldn't catch their breath easily. Her bones ached like muscles should after hard-strain (because there were tumors there too) and she lived so nauseous that even the anti-nausea drugs did nothing to relieve her. She lost 15 pounds in a week from throwing up so often. When we weren't around, she cried, because she knew her time was ticking down faster than she wanted.

We scheduled wedding dress shopping around Mom's appointments. At the time I was living in Maryland and she and the rest of the family were living in Florida. She had chemo on Monday, but usually felt good on Tuesday until the evening. By Wednesday she was knocked out with sickness. I flew down on Sunday night. We looked through magazines while she was hooked up to her port sitting in a large blue chair. Monitors beeped. The elderly man beside us snored through his treatment. Nurses in scrubs and foam shoes moved about.

The next day all the girls loaded up early to go try on real dresses. Not pictures on a screen, but fabric and zippers and consultants. Even knowing that I'm not much of a "feeler," I had really looked forward to standing on a little pedestal with my mom and sisters (and maybe a few close friends) while becoming speckled red in (rare) tearful confidence: "This is my dress!" I imagined Mom misty, too. I wanted to feel those things I'd heard just about everybody else describe. The most concern I had in my imagining of that moment was of maybe being body-self-conscious or not liking my hair or something silly.

Mom booked our first appointment at a discount bridal chain so I could try on silhouettes and see what I liked. We stopped for a slimming, magical breakfast of fast food drive-thru and ate our sausage biscuits in front of the salon waiting for our appointment. Mom was so excited. She couldn't eat, but she sipped on water and scrolled through my internet boards one more time. When we walked in the door she grabbed all the dress catalogues they had on display and excitedly started looking through them, showing me ones she thought I would like. I tried on about 8 or 9 dresses that hour, completely unaware that almost every time I disappeared into the dressing room Mom had to excuse herself to the bathroom to throw-up bile and dry heave. Each time I walked out of the white swinging door, she was sitting there smiling at me. Years later I found out that she had told my sisters, who obviously saw her running to the bathroom, not to tell me. She didn't want to ruin my experience and fun.

The week I got engaged, my dad — on her behalf, but not because she asked him to — had to sit me down and have an uncomfortably, completely-right conversation about my focus during wedding planning. My enthusiasm and "dream!" was breaking her heart. She would have roped the moon for me, but she couldn't imagine how she could help me pull off such an elaborate, detailed plan given how sick she was. "Don't you dare make your mother feel bad. She shouldn't be telling me how sorry she feels. This wedding is not all about you. And neither will your marriage be. Because life isn't all about you. We are so excited for you and Caleb, and we want to give you a special day filled with happiness. But your mother is fighting for her life and you need to more than remember that — you need to focus on that. We don't know what the next few weeks and months are going to hold for her, for us, but you are going to have to have a new dream: Mom being at your wedding, even if that means driving to a courthouse and having dinner in Tarpon Springs afterwards. I wish this wasn't our reality, and I'm so sorry for all of us that it is. But it is. And this isn't going to be The Kristen Bride Show, this is going to be a time of caring about others more than ourself." I cried as I knew he was right but it was emotional to hear. This was harder for Mom than it was for me. She wasn't going to help plan my wedding shower like she had always dreamed. This was indeed a time to hone in on "the big stuff" and let everything else blow away in the breeze.

We finished at the first dress shop and Mom drove us to the second salon of the day. Except she had made a little mistake — the acclaimed, designer "experience" salon was down by the beach. Apparently they had multiple stores, but the mall location, which we were at, was 95% prom dresses with about 12 off-the-rack wedding dresses in the back. It was purple and hot-pink with disco balls and lots of feathers. Not exactly the high-end bridal market.

At this point in the day I was noticing that Mom was walking slowly and looking green. She felt awful that we had gone to the wrong place and promised me that we could still go to the real boutique. "Do you want to just look at the dresses we have here?" the friendly employee asked. "Sure!" Mom made the effort to come all this way...let's try on some gowns.

I grabbed three dresses that looked nothing like what I wanted, but I thought would at least be worth the stop. The first didn't fit at all, the second barely fit so I waddled out in it. All my sisters and Mom were waiting for me, but within 30 seconds I was back in the fitting room because it had earned a big fat thumbs down. The last dress, in my estimation, was frumpy, boring, and I probably shouldn't waste everyone's time. But the employee convinced me to just try. So I did. Aaaaand it looked just as boring, frumpy, and baggy on me. Blech. "Let's look at it out in the showroom! It'll give you a better perspective!"

With a face I imagine being almost bratty and "just so annoyed," I marched unenthused out of the dressing room, shaking my head "Nope" — only to find my sisters and Mom all gone. In their place sat a high school boy I'd never seen before. "Hey, I'm Katie's friend. I saw she was here and I'm on lunch-break so I came over to say hi." "Oh, well, hello. Nice to meet you...Do you know where my sisters and mom are?" "Uh, no. They just told me to wait here." A minute or so later they returned. Mom was really, really not doing well. She leaned on Katie and Katie gave me "time to stop" eyes. They'd been in the bathroom and Mom couldn't hide it anymore.

I stood in the mirror while the store employee worked furiously to make a sale — pinning, clipping, rolling, tucking — rearranging the dress and showing how it could fit with some alterations. It was definitely getting better but was certainly not a "wow!" moment inside me. I turned around to show it to my weakened Mom and her eyes lit up. "Oh that's definitely my favorite of the day. Don't you love it?!" Ummm. "It's everything you wanted." And there it was.

Everything I wanted.

Right in front of my eyes: Mom and my sisters to be a part of this with me, even if they weren't fully understanding how significant it was. The new dream. Flexible. Letting go.

I made a decision to wear a dress on my wedding day, because my mom was a part of the moment -- giving so much of herself to be there. I sometimes feel a little twinge when I watch "pick the dress" shows and see a bride get that lump of happiness and putter in tears, with a posse of cheering women behind her. But I would do it all over again.

I wore a perfectly lovely gown that didn't exactly make me sparkle inside and you know what? I was really happy. I walked down the aisle of a local wedding venue, on a boggy-hot Thursday in the dead of August, because the venue had no weekends available until the following year and, well, we just didn't have that kind of time. In my wedding dress, I married the love of my life; and my mom was sitting there watching me. She was wearing a wig and an arm compression brace and glasses — because chemo made her eyes itch and so did eye make-up. We got ready at my parent's home in the big room over the garage, in the room my mom died in 17 months later. Friends and family were scattered all over the region in hotels and good peoples' houses.

***

Guests came from north, south, east, and west. Some on planes, some in caravan. Some from hundreds, some from thousands of miles away. I knew I was looking forward to everyone coming to town, but somehow in all the planning it hadn't registered that they would all be here at the same time, in the flesh! Everyone all together. We hadn't really thought through "the plan" for when they all got in two nights before the wedding and happened to show up at my parents' house to see us. Quickly my dad jumped into action and ran off to the grocery store, while my grandma started making macaroni salad. Within the hour they had a whole BBQ feast laid out. The rooms and yard of the house were teeming with extended family. A volleyball game started up. The deck was crowded. The food smelled so good. Caleb and I ran off for ten minutes all "Whaaat is this?! This is so crazy!" The Olympics were turned on and we watched the US win gold in the pool. I could have thrown my dress on and gotten married that evening and had "the best wedding ever." I caught my dad with some uncles in the side yard playing bocce ball.

I would have missed it all. Me and my stupid stubborn self-importance would have ruined the most pure baptism of love I've ever experienced. Had I been rigid, I could have gotten my way. I could have forced it to happen. And I think there would have been some sweet memories. But God is up to our good. "A man's heart plans his way, but the Lord directs his steps." The desire for a meaningful, memorable wedding event was not stupid or selfish, but clinging to my very limited version of what could be meaningful and memorable was. He's just so far beyond us. He desires to give us more than we want to give ourselves.

He's so smart. He's so able. And, my, did Mom live in that. She let her heart flex when the plans changed. She adapted and admitted when she was wrong. She excellently lived out faith, which changes everything. Rules and over-control and forsaking and hiding — these destroy what is meant to be the richest, best parts of life. Flexibility gave her fullness. She had the ability to accept her boundary lines and genuinely find the good in whatever they were. The lie of legalism — of itty-bitty, detailed spiritual rigidity — is that there is one more required step, that you have to take care of one more thing, and then... Then it will be all right. No, Mom knew all was well. All would be well. She wasn't in charge and Someone very qualified was. Therefore she could relax and say "It's okay! We will figure it out!" She was right.

What Mama Bear Taught Me About…

7. EMOTIONS

"And I urge you to please notice when you are happy, and exclaim or murmur or think at some point, 'If this isn't nice, I don't know what is.'"
— Kurt Vonnegut

One of Pixar's latest masterpieces is the creative and insightful film "Inside Out." If you haven't seen it, the idea is that human beings experience five main emotions (and all other emotions are simply various blends): anger, fear, disgust, sadness, and joy. In this movie the emotions are personified and are literally tiny creatures inside a human being's head, controlling the thoughts and feelings from the main headquarters of the brain. There are charming details like an actual Train of Thought with tracks across the mind and Dream Works, the small budget studio where our nightly dreams are directed like outlandish independent films.

The message of the movie is that joy and sadness need each other, and a main story line is that we all have these golden "core memories" that have shaped who we are and what we love. Memories are represented by colorful, marble-like balls that are stored and organized in the brain. For some reason certain memories stand out and establish themselves while other ones seem fully to disappear. After the movie I couldn't resist analyzing elements of what I had just seen and trying to identify what my own core memories are. I came up with many (not five or six like the movie suggests), and a significant one revolves around the emotional sensitivity I remember having as a young girl.

I have specific recall of being in our Flower Hill neighborhood grocery store and taking in the people around me. I paid close attention to the body language, facial expressions, and "energy" a person emanated. I was only about eight years old, but I was extremely aware of the vibes and condition of shoppers around me.

While gathering tomatoes into a plastic sack, a hunched, petite, weary old man across the produce-bin caught my attention. He had a wrinkled, hound-dog face and looked plain sad. His under-eyes hung like sun-faded swag curtains. When he shuffled across the floor in his black, soft, velcro shoes all that could be heard was the gentle puff of air the foam soles exhaled. His grey hair, ashy pants, and cloudy shirt were the colors of down-in-the-dumps. As he finished loading his basket he slowly unfolded a soft, tired paper list then looked up with an Eeyore expression in the direction of the cash register, as if thinking: "Oh bother, I have to go all the way over there. Sigh." I spied him through the onion pile. And my heart cracked like a paint stir-stick. Ooof. I felt sad with him. I had such an urge to run over and hug, reassure, and connect with him. "It's going to be okay!" I hoped. He went on his way and I on mine but I couldn't resist praying as I walked the store. "God, please make that man smile today. Just help him feel really happy. I know You are good, so please let him know that too. Can You cheer him up?"

Whenever I saw an ambulance or fire truck pass, my heart sank and I felt queasy for loved ones. I'd pray "Oh Lord, protect the people involved. Save their lives and do miracles. Whatever happened, please keep them safe and their families together."

***

My life was a blessed one, in that I had the privilege of being a carefree child in a warm home. I played and my imagination was vibrant. I felt safe with my parents and didn't spend time pondering "anything wrong." We weren't rich, but we always had food in the kitchen and I never feared the roof staying over our heads. But, as my first decade came to a close and the second one began, I started to change. My grandmother was rediagnosed with cancer. We moved across the country to California, which was exciting but it did make me feel nervous. My familiar, tight community was a critical part of life, and leaving it, even at nine years old, seemed quite big.

Moving a family of six 3,000 miles is stressful and that process is my first memory of my parents fighting. After making the adjustments and being "the new girl" for the first time in my life — I had never not had friends! — I was grateful and attached to a small but sweet group of girls I really enjoyed. Life in California felt like one big, long vacation and my parents looked and acted the happiest I had ever seen them. But then my dad's workplace went bankrupt. Within months of moving, there was talk of going back to Maryland. I was so disappointed. I could tell the cares of the world were weighing on my parents' shoulders.

In the midst of this, the family all caught an awful case of scabies, and the medicine treating it ended up causing my mom's first miscarriage (she didn't know she was pregnant when she took it). I saw my dad sob for the first time. Right before our move back to Maryland was final, Mom found out she was pregnant (and therefore very sick) again. Dad commuted across the country for a couple of months. Once in Maryland we lived out of a friend's basement until we could get a house of our own. My grandmother died from cancer not long after and I saw my mom weep for the first time. And second time. And third time. And… and…

***

"When I was a girl, my life was music that was always getting louder.
Everything moved me. A dog following a stranger. That made me feel so much. A
calendar that showed the wrong month. I could have cried over it. I did. Where
the smoke from a chimney ended. How an overturned bottle rested at the edge
of a table. I spent my life learning to feel less. Every day I felt less. Is that
growing old? Or is it something worse? You cannot protect yourself from
sadness without protecting yourself from happiness."
–Jonathan Safran Foer

Emotions had now pressed right up in my face, socially-unacceptably close
with shameless disregard for my "personal space," and I was flustered by
them. I could smell their breath. I wasn't used to the uneasy feeling of what I
can now name: vulnerability. Exposed. Like a duck all alone on the open lake
during hunting season. Being a strong person was my MO. When emotions
wrapped their arms around my neck and screeched in my face like a manic
little monkey, kicking its feet on my chest and freaking me out, I turned my
internal nose upward and ignored them. Tuned them out. Tossed them
ignominiously through the swinging saloon doors. These will not get the best
of me! Sticks and stones may break my bones, but these damn things will not
hurt me!

It was in the middle of my 10th year that my mom gave birth to Dude, her
"angel from heaven"-baby that kept her tethered to the good in life on earth
and the better life to come. The day I met that boy was a core memory for me.
He and Mom were laying on her lightly-stained wooden bed with blue-and-
white-checkered sheets. He had a head full of dark hair, bubble lips, and
beignet puffed cheeks.

He was hours old, and physically seeing him with my eyes was love at first
sight. I believe in it! It's impossible to forget the way your heart swells with
the most pleasant lukewarm water and then bursts like a balloon too full. You

feel it stream down past your hips pooling at your feet. My breath was taken away and I experienced tunnel vision. Family friends took us "big kids" for the evening, but within minutes of arriving I asked if I could go back home. They let me and I spent the whole night laying next to Dude's sleeping, kitty body and staring. After this it was a long time before I felt so innocently and completely again. It is true, of course, that you can't turn your nose from sadness without also turning it from happiness.

***

The Meyers-Briggs Personality Theory came into my life post-high-school. If I thought I loved "picking up on vibes" and trying to figure people out before, I now arrived at my people-watching Mecca with these new personality-dissecting tools! I began quizzing everyone I knew, eager to learn and discuss what made us all tick, in our own distinctive ways. To me it felt like the ultimate conversation starter, to analyze myself, as well as the people I loved. Of course these methods weren't "everything" but they seemed like a great foundation for understanding each other.

Even though we were close, likely best, friends I thought that Mom would have been a "T" for "Thinker," not an "F" for "Feeler." Being as wise, self-controlled, and discerning as she was—she fooled me! After hearing her answers to the many questions I found myself asking her, I regularly exclaimed, "Really?! Are you sure?!" to the point where she laughed. "Yes, I am SURE! You don't think I am a liar, too, do you??" I had incorrectly assumed that "feelers" were all dramatic, theatric, and "had no control." Mom taught me this was not so. And, of course, personality theories are greatly limited.

Labels make things "black and white" that are actually colorful. I understand that personality-spectrums are not the entire picture, and Mom just might have been the most balanced "Thinker-Feeler" I've ever known! But this obsession did help me to know her more fully and to hear her uncomfortably share some strong feelings that she had always, for whatever reason (maturity, our protection, doubt, busyness, what have you), kept hush-hush.

***

To be frankly personal about this hero of a woman: Mom felt like such a failure as a mother. She also felt like she had tried as hard as she possibly could to engage, learn, implement, and love. For example, she longed for us kids to be close all through our lives. She looked fondly—and discouragedly— at families with children who were "such best friends!" "What else could I have done?," she'd wonder. "I prayed...maybe not enough? I made you play together...Maybe I should have let you have more space? I made you apologize and address each other...Maybe I should have let you sort it out yourselves? Did I just raise mean people? Am I a mean person?" In reflecting, she'd describe to me her mother and her family and her cozy reflections of simple enjoyment of each other's company. "I wanted that so badly for you guys. I really did."

When she'd let her horrible little monkey out of its cage for me too see, I felt bad for her, but I didn't see things the way she did. "We do love each other, Mom!" my mind would instantly affirm. I mean, yeah, we're kind of blunt and rough with each other and we are sometimes mean; but I think we're fine! You know, in a Beverly Hillbillies kind of way! We're motley...nuthin' wrong with that!

My memories of childhood are full of dodgeball games and handstand competitions with Timmy, after making spaghetti for lunch every single day when we were homeschooled together. My memories are full of making up dances with Katie (and then entire shows!) and practicing for hours in our many costumes. Start the cassette tape. Pause. Rewind. Start again. Pause. Rewind. My memories are building teepees and forts in the woods, making the Home Owner's Association mad because of all the tree limbs we snapped off, and "catching crawdads" in the creek (even though we mostly just walked from rock to rock, feeling so cool and independent-ish).

I remember dozens of scenes riding bikes, playing manhunt, swimming at the pool, beating levels of Frogger together, singing karaoke-style to the Tarzan soundtrack while doing dishes, having the big kids make the little kids laugh or do tricks, getting in trouble because we were staying up too late talking to each other in our bunk and trundle beds when we were supposed to be going to sleep. My memories are all of us at T-ball, soccer, basketball, flag football, karate, volleyball, and school plays — in seats cheering for whoever was in the spotlight that hour. My memories are of family dinner, around the table, hands held for prayers, far more often than not.

One of my all-time favorite core memories was the most perfect autumn day when we minivan-ed over to a local fall festival. The trees were orange, the pumpkins were orange, the sunset was orange. We played together in the hay-bale maze until the light turned blue and the air felt like the air conditioning had just been turned on. I remember seeing Mom in the passenger seat, leaning her weight towards Dad, elbow on the left side armrest; and I remember catching glimpses of their happy eyes in the rearview mirror looking back at us. Timmy was in a particularly goofy mood and was making us all laugh. It was perfect. I remember thinking it then. Now, I know it was true.

***

That's the problem I have with feelings, though. They are valid, and "real" but they are beyond our easy understanding and they often seem to conflict with one another. It may be true you feel a particular way, but it doesn't mean what you feel is true. I know my mom was not a failure of a mother. But I know it is true that she often felt like one. Her feelings were valid, they were real feelings, but they weren't an accurate or complete gauge of herself. Logic and simple reason became fast friends of mine because it was easy to say, "Ah, you feel how? Well that is wrong. Let me show you data and facts to prove to you what is true." This was how I navigated myself and the world around me. I could so easily move from "Don't believe your feelings, they are not dependable!" to "Do not feel your feelings, they are not worthwhile" — without meaning to. No one taught me that! But it's the natural place to which the path of ignoring our God-given emotions leads us.

What was true mattered. Feeling lonely didn't matter because I knew for a fact I was not alone. People — good loving people — were everywhere in my life! "You are not alone." I'd tell myself. "So do not feel alone. You. Do. Not. Feel. Alone." I knew so well who I believed I should be or who I wanted to be, that I denied the truth of who I was. This mind over matter prowess became a source of pride to me. And it was addicting. I liked the superior position that it appeared to give me in life. "Those people" who couldn't manage themselves were weaker, in my estimation.

***

A sensation I particularly hate is the feeling of throwing up. (Quick note: I apologize for how much vomiting is written about in this book. It's so...unsavory and crude! It might sound crazy, but it has truly been one of the hardest and greatest life lessons and analogies for me. So thanks for bearing with me.) I was prone to car and sea sickness my whole life, and I caught the common winter stomach flu an average amount as a kid. But my sophomore year of high school, as a round of the bug was passing through, I made the decision not to throw up. I do not like it, no not one little bit! I will not do it, I said with grit.

I could feel the early rumbling around bedtime, so I parked myself on the couch and turned on the TV to distract my mind. As the night wore on I could hear the victims upstairs succumbing to their fate, and it only empowered my decision. I made the mistake of laying down on the couch as I got tired, but I quickly learned my lesson and stayed sitting upright the rest of the night. The nausea would grow and my mouth (that hideous warning flag) would fill with saliva. I would calmly take a bite out of a lime popsicle and let it melt on my tongue, while I closed my eyes and focused on 'my truth': I will not throw up. A couple of times I got off the couch, holding my stomach, and paced around barefoot outside on the snow-covered deck, smelling the smoky-fireplace, nighttime air, and concentrating on how much my feet burned in the snow. Guys. Even typing this I'm shaking my head. Goodness. As the sun started to rise, I let go of the last bits of stamina left, letting them blow away like dandelion-wishes in the wind. I fell asleep (upright) and did it. I survived the worst part and chowed through a few more lime popsicles before the 24 hour mark arrived; but I did not throw up!

Similarly, when I needed to get my first cavity drilled I declined the Novocaine because I just do not like shots or needles. I don't do it. It freaks me out. I can't turn my nose to it. It is an Achilles heel. So I skip it as much as possible! "Pain is just feeling," I reminded myself. As I laid on the taupe medical chair, with bright light and white bib on me, I tuned out the smell of drill burning through enamel. I tuned out the sensitivity, as it moved closer to the core nerve rod in my tooth, feeling merely like when you drink water that is too cold and your teeth ache. Then, when drill actually met nerve, I dug my finger nails into my palms and counted to ten. "You can do anything for 10 seconds," my mom used to tell me. Usually before "eight" they would pause and readjust or rinse before resuming work, and I would start back at "one."

I read a meme once that said, "Not sure if I'm emotionally strong and can handle anything...or if I'm a heartless sociopath." I've hardly ever related to a pondering more! I feel like my mind has been on overdrive for years, while my heart has been in a blue plastic bin in the basement. I prided myself on not being a crier and worked to keep the basement door locked real tight. Throughout middle and high school I only remember a handful of tears: finding out Mom had miscarried, one night about two months into my mom having cancer when I was stressed, another night as I thought about Mom dying, and after we lost the league basketball championship in my senior year. "Crying means you cared," my mom tried to comfort me as I felt so sad about losing and so embarrassed to feel so sad. "Caring is a good, good thing."

***

As my second decade came to a close, plates began to shift under my surface once again and soul quakes were on the brink. At age 19, floodgates of feeling opened —during my first real heartbreak. Part of why it hurt so badly was because I didn't even realize myself how much I cared...until things had fallen apart. It was the first season of my life where I couldn't willfully out-muscle the tears. This experience was very much a "lightbulb" season and a brand new chapter in my little life story. It wasn't about a boy, it was about everything. God, decision, desire, worldview, thought process, connection, purpose, faith — even about emotion. By the time I was 20, I could at least acknowledge that maybe it was a bit unhealthy to be as (seemingly) unfeeling as I was.

A family situation arose where one of "the kids" was greatly mistreated, and the child involved wasn't entirely innocent in the matter, but had definitely been wronged by people who were deliberate and should have known better. People my family had trusted. My mom emotionally unraveled and the stitches of her composure popped open. She just couldn't stop crying and she couldn't stop feeling the pain of it so deeply. She got stuck at the grocery store once because she was unable to calm down and Dad had to go pick her up.

This happened during Thanksgiving, and I remember looking around the table during the holiday feast and noticing how swollen both of my parents' faces were. I felt guilty for being callous. Mom asked me once that week how I was carrying on so normally. I had nothing to say, other than something about God making beauty from ashes and it'll be alright. "He has a plan!" I silver-lined. The moment I became aware of the situation, it was if my whole torso and everything in it disconnected from me. I switched the light off from neck to hips. Nothing to see, nothing to feel here! Move right along! This response was concerning. What is the matter with me? I secretly wondered.

***

I met Caleb just after my 21st birthday and I'll never ever forget the first time we had The Feelings conversation: "Do you…ever…wonder…or, uh, feel like…you have a hard time with…emotions? Like, not because they're too much but, like, because they're missing?" I watched his eyes closely and when I finished my stammering they immediately said: "Oh thank God, you too!" Then he verbally said, "Yes, definitely. You do too?!" This was such a relieving and exciting commonality and exchange between us. Shocker of shockers: admitting it to each other made us feel closer, and happier together. Weird, hey?

When I finally worked up the courage to tell my mom "I think I'm a freak," she looked sincerely tickled. "Oh, no no no. This is much more common than you realize." Is it?! Are you sure?! "I'm very sure," she assured. This made me feel quite better. Her final year, especially, we bonded — with knowing smirks — over the ways our family was feeling its way through the whole situation of losing her.

Caleb and I were living with the baby in the basement apartment of my parent's house, and one night I left our king-sized bed downstairs and traveled up two flights to sit next to my parents' king-sized bed. "Are you up?"

I whispered to Mom. "Mmmhhm" and she set her hand on top of mine. In the dark I stumbled through some feelings. "I just want you to know that I really hate that you are sick. I'm sorry I don't cry all the time about it or, I don't know, I don't know how I'm supposed to be. But I don't want you to feel like it doesn't bother me. I really, really hate it. I don't want you to go." She was very strong with me and said she knew, and was proud of me, and wished she could stay longer. She also told me that my obsession with selling baby clothes online was enough for her. This made me laugh. I was totally coping with my sadness by the emotional-high of making an instant sale!

My longtime career has been photography, which I love! But it is a methodical, drawn-out process. You book a job weeks or months or even over a year in advance. You shoot. You go home to look at the pictures. You edit later. Then you deliver the images, generally after being paid. Selling clothes had a Wall-Street-esque rush to it. I'd generate a big stink with my followers/customers about the sale. I'd get everything lined up in order, and at exactly the previously announced time I'd "go go go!" posting outfit by outfit, watching the sales come in! It's ridiculous but my heart would race and I'd get this adrenaline shot that I found irresistible. Mom was clever enough to see that I was finding a joy in this that I really needed, because I was hurting greatly in other places. "You have your online sales, and Dad has his backyard," she teased that night.

Dad had a similar strange compulsion take him over during this time. We always have had dozens of "things to work on at the house." Caleb and Tim were chipping away at my parents' various projects and Dad was always leading the pack. They were all dedicated to finishing a wrap-around porch for Mom — something that had always been her dream for a home and had never happened. She had also always wanted a white, French country kitchen. They had made the kitchen happen, so now it was porch time.

Halfway through this project, however, Dad had an *If You Give A Mouse A Cookie* moment. Having Tim cut down some limbs in the woods beside our house, turned into Caleb and Tim cutting down some trees in the woods beside our house, which turned into creating a clearing to enlarge the yard, which turned into planting grass, and setting up a fire pit. The whole project consumed their free time, particularly Dad's. It was precious to see him out there fostering his little baby grass shoots. He'd lug out the hose and sprinklers and stand out there surveying his hard work growing before his eyes. Mom said that it was a subconscious way of being able to control life, to make something become and stay alive. She knew it was bringing him so much joy, which did amuse her but she also said it shouted how much he cared, which meant everything to her.

***

Mom had long ago come to terms with "embracing feelings." Where I had denial, she had acceptance. She was dazzling in how she didn't resist what came her way. As a ship rides atop both stormy water or still peace, so did she. I really do view her as the beautiful, steady, carved figurehead sailing ever onward as lightning strikes, waves heave, and the crew scrambles on the deck floor. With peace, with confidence, without flinching, she led the way. "You just have to go throw up, Kristen. Don't fight it. You're just going to make yourself more miserable."

Mom kept a close watch on herself, and without ever hearing verbiage like "self-care," I watched her take life in stride without tuning out the intensity. For example, one of my favorite Mom-stories was one night in the middle of the school week, during basketball season. We had come home late from an away game and the kitchen hadn't been picked up from breakfast. Uniforms had to be washed for tomorrow and procrastinating students were overreacting to all this homework! It's not faaaaair! Naked babies were running through the halls, and all of a sudden we realized we hadn't seen Mom in a little while. "Mom! Mom! Mom! Where are you? Mom?" We eventually found her in our kid's bathroom. She had locked herself in with a bowl of ice cream, a plastic cup of navy paint, and some stamps. She had started a nautical theme in there but had never gotten around to her vision of adding stars and stripes to the part of the wall below the chair rail. "I needed to do something creative," she said as if she were telling us the time. "Oh. Alright. Well. How long will you be in here?" we wondered. "I'm not sure," she smiled. That was so Mom.

On another stressful day, ten minutes before we were supposed to be heading out the door, one of the boys saw her coming into the house with a buzzsaw. For dramatic flair, but with a pinch of concern, he came Paul Revere-ing up the stairs "Guyyys! Mom has a saw! Mom has a saw!" I told everyone to make themselves disappear and to let me see what was going on. I found her in the kitchen cutting a table in half. Our family was too big to fit around a normal dinner table, so she was thrilled to find two identical tables at a flea market that she could cover with one big tablecloth to look like one nice, big, farm style table. However, once in the house, she realized the two tables side-by-side were a bit too long for the space she was working with. She decided to trim the ends off one of the tables to make a custom fit. Two years went by and she had never touched it, but all of a sudden inspiration struck at 2:55 on a November Tuesday afternoon. It was her way of not blowing up, not doing something she regretted, listening to her feelings, but not being their slave. A quick creative break, that's all! Don't fight it! You'll just make yourself miserable!

She taught me much on this facet of life while she lived, but since she's been gone I really feel as if the dots have started to connect for me. When I reminisce or "go back" to life with her, I am nearly always struck with the measured, perceptive, observational thinking she did and how her powerful, colorful, expressed emotions fit so nicely together. Like salt and pepper. She could regulate herself, but not by self-neglect. And she could "have the feels," without overreacting as a way of life. She could talk herself down off the ledge without pretending there was no ledge. In reflection I clearly see how she lived with her heart nerve-endings sensitive, but processed the sensations through her brain. Mom made such a point of noticing — and extending the offer for me to notice — the most soul-filling bits of life.

***

This was perhaps one of the Top Three qualities I loved most about my mom: she was eager and constant when it came to identifying how she felt, and she was expressively vocal about it when what she was feeling was up-lifting. I know it's very important to engage and deal with negative emotions and not "throw a rug over a rattlesnake." We see the writers in Scripture (Jesus Himself!) spend detailed, poetic pages unpacking just how miserable or down they felt — sometimes for chapters and chapters. They went deep into their souls, even in the dark times.

The griefs are important. But I think there is something particularly life-giving about having eyes that wander for things to be grateful for, to feel happy about. For things that will spread sweetness. For the "shooting star" seconds that you chose not to miss and that bring richness to your day. The way a heavy zipper feels on an expensive purse. The way your legs feel just after you've shaved. Catching eye-contact with a stranger in public. A really productive nose blow. Holding a baby's head in the palm of your hand. A bite of salad with the perfect amount of toppings in the same bite. Pulling into your driveway at night and the way the headlights shine on the house. Getting the letter or email containing results or news you've been waiting for and reading really fast while muttering under your breath. Finding something you lost when you weren't looking for it. The display of flowers at the grocery store. The smell of chlorine the moment you walk through a pool locker room. Having more money on a gift card than you thought. These are all things I remember my mom noticing, pointing out to me (briefly), and just... liking. Just... feeling.

PS I'm doing much better. I've cried, like, three times this month, so, yeehaw!

What Mama Bear Taught Me About…

8. MAGIC MOMENTS

"Of course there must be lots of Magic in the world,' he said wisely one day, 'but people don't know what it is like or how to make it. Perhaps the beginning is just to say nice thing are going to happen until you make them happen."
--Frances Hodgson Burnett

As I'm writing, there is a recent, viral post online regarding a young man's first days of work at Target. He typed out and shared about 12-15 interactions with customers he had throughout the day. Some were funny, some were bizarre, some were sweet, some were pretty average and boring. But all strung together in a list, they were charming and heart-touching, as millions shared his original post. Similarly, the internet nearly exploded recently at the happy antics of a middle aged mom who bought a Star Wars mask. She recorded herself putting it on (as she sat in her car, presumably waiting for her kids to get out of school) and she was positively tickled. Seeing her face through the eyes of this clever mask was simply too much for her. She laughed with all her might, from deep in her belly, and then she roared again and would finally go silent in glee — only to start all over again! People were happily captivated watching her, resonating with the goodness of such uncontainable joy in a simple, silly part of a normal day.

***

"He who can no longer pause to wonder and stand rapt in awe is as good as dead, his eyes are closed."
–Albert Einstein

My husband, Caleb, has recently transitioned from being a construction contractor to being a full-time musician. He books weddings and events here and there, but his normal workday consists of standing on a street corner, playing his violin to all who pass by. We've been amazed at the interactions this creates. There was a grown man wearing khakis, a red polo shirt, and black work shoes. His dark hair was parted on the side and he had the sort of belly that might be flat if its owner stood up straight and sucked it in, but — at ease — it sat sleepily on the sill of his pants. With one hand he held his smartphone and with the other hand he held his face as he wept. Tears streaming, with gasps and trembling. It was quite a sight! The crowd of about 20 other vacationers watching Caleb at the time seemed not to notice the man in the back corner — his heart pouring out of his eyes.

Another day Caleb was playing at a downtown farmer's market in San Diego. A grandmotherly, pleasantly-plump, devoutly-Catholic, hispanic woman stood for 10 minutes or so gazing, hands gently laid over her heart. She saw that I was Caleb's wife, and she came over to talk to me. She struggled with her phone as she tried to find pictures to help tell her story in broken-English. Tragedy, loss, a little girl she loved, and redemption came stumbling out as she explained to me how certain songs "take me right to heaven, and all is well." She patted her palm over her heart again and then lifted it to the sky with her eyes closed.

A young janitor at a nearby restaurant was taking his work break and sat in the grass. He was completely blank-faced and quiet. Thirty minutes later he returned to his shift. A couple of hours later, with his workday behind him, he was back on the grass where he stayed for two more hours. Caleb wrapped up after dark; and the young man, who had displayed no emotion, quietly approached Caleb. "Thank you for giving me your gift. I needed it today." And then he was gone.

A personal favorite character of mine was a head-turning 40-something-year-old lady who had sass, spunk, and the most eccentric, curly hair to match her bold persona. She seemed to be dressed almost like a toddler: just putting on whatever were her favorites and preferences in the moment, not necessarily because the individual items contributed to a "complete ensemble." Someone, it truly appeared, who really doesn't care what other people think and is utterly comfortable being her own person. Red shoes, fanny pack (accentuating her pear shape), a beaded vest, big lips colored in with pink, long loose shorts, eyes "as big as saucers," and fair skin — all assembled to compose her style.

As Caleb concluded a song, she clapped and hollered and immediately went up to lavish praise on him and tell him about her years in choir. As he began to play the next song, without asking or hesitating, she stood beside Caleb and sang along — as if the two of them were performing for everyone else! I describe her without the smallest bit of mockery (Amusement? Definitely.) because I was impressed with her! "Man," I thought, "that takes serious guts!" Granted, I'm a horrible singer; but regardless, I can't imagine joining a group of strangers in a large public area and jumping right into a live, uninvited, impromptu performance! I really don't think I could or would do it! What a fascinating, confident human being I'm witnessing right now! After a song or two, she came over to me and fawned over the kids and our family. Then she opened up about her life-long desire to have a family of her own, but confessed that she thinks she scares men away. "It might not be in the cards for me. But I'm glad to see you're enjoying your family. It's a great thing to have, I hope you know."

One of Caleb's most meaningful memories is of a tight, toned, bald man who looked like he would own a mud-race franchise. The guy was kindly inquisitive about how Caleb got into "this" (music, street music, etc). Caleb explained that mostly he wanted to find a way to do what he loved if it could support his family, especially if it freed him up to spend more time with us. The kids and I were sitting nearby. On the spot, he bought one of Caleb's CDs and briefly explained that he was in the beginning of launching his own small business, specifically to change the dynamic of his family life and spend more time with the wife and kids he loved so much. He wanted to give Caleb a hug and then he moved along. But less then 10 minutes later the man was back. He passed through in the middle of a song, dropped an $100 bill in the bucket, and mouthed to Caleb, "Go get 'em."

***

One of the most unexpected, sweet parts of being pregnant and then, especially, having a baby is how it draws affection out of the woodwork. I've lived on the "aggressive northeast coast" most of my life and generally adhere to the notion that "Someone who smiles too much has something to hide." Of course this isn't fully true, but when I'm out and about and I see someone extremely and noisily jovial, my first sensation is skepticism. On the other hand, people who are quiet or distant or reserved in public don't seem rude to me at all. Now, any kind of warm, thoughtful gesture or effort is refreshing, I think. Don't get me wrong. I'm just very accustomed to and familiar with a fast-paced, mind your business, tell-it-like-it-is culture. So, when I had a baby in this culture I was pleasantly surprised by all the sweetness that began to sneak out of my tough-spined neighbors. I'm still surprised at each gangly, teenage waiter-boy or tight-lipped, hair-sprayed "Miss Piggy" or polished, crispy business man that comes out of his or her shell because...the baby!

In life, these sacred people-moments are accompanied by the simple magic of little surprises, happy coincidences, or the art of inanimate remnants. Discovering a toy set-up that was abandoned by a child at play. (Currently on the floor of my bedroom is a road made out of children's books, paved for a yellow pick up truck. There is a plastic triceratops riding in the truck bed.) Or a curious tone of voice (like when a large, gruff man has a high-pitched, soft voice. It's surprising!) Or noticing a person sitting in a coffee shop, but clearly checking the time waiting for someone to meet them. Or when there is the perfect amount of cheese, meat, and cracker to finish off your snack gratifyingly. Or when you see 77,777 or 12,345 or any such configuration on the odometer. Or when your hair is long enough to be in a pony tail and you happen to be wearing a shirt that allows the end of your hair to brush across your back. Or the first morning you wake up and it feels like spring — it's felt like winter for so long but not today: today, for a few early hours, it feels like spring.

Magic moments. They enrich our lives. Nothing groundbreaking, or deeply theological. These moments are nothing worth naming a chapter over in your life book. Yet, they're the descriptors and the symbolism. My mom lived poised to be moved by the big and the small. She was available and ready for her heart to be touched, just about anywhere. My rumblings in this chapter may not be much different than what I have shared about emotions, other than this: I believe you have to want to feel and find magic moments. Don't just like them in theory, but look for them. Hunt them down. Children have the blessing of being naturally full of wonder. As we stiffen and worry, our imaginations get crusty and worlds of play, story, and simple thrill eludes us. I think it's the rare adult, in my experience, that is full of pure wonder. My mom was one of them, as she wanted to be. She watched for hidden delights with intention.

I desperately miss her little observations. Her radar rarely missed random, interesting scenes. At the sight of a stranger in her favorite colors, she'd lean in and say "Ooo! Now that is the palette I love most!" When food arrived, she would pause significantly, close her eyes, and breath in the aroma before eating a single bite. A moment of anticipation before indulging. She loved sharpening her mind with Sudoku and crosswords puzzles and checking our math homework (without the answer key). "When you start to get old, you can really feel your brain working hard in there. It gets rusty!" she'd explain.

Once at the grocery store she was frozen in her tracks because the color of an eggplant took her breath away. And Mom wasn't this airy, fluff, melodramatic woman! No, she was a bear! She had concrete behind her will, her whole neck would splotch red when she was mad, and her eyes could shoot bullets. She was opinionated, stubborn, and craved being challenged. She would bend ear to the carpet to squint through the bottom crack of a bedroom door, to spy on a toddler playing in his own little world after a nap. She used to talk about our skin — how Katie had the most stretchy skin she'd ever seen. ("It's like there was elastic injected into her! You really could hold her up like a puppy in your fist by grabbing the skin on her back!") She marveled at Lauren's upper arms, because her skin was just the perfect density to squeeze or hold your cheek to.

Now I'm realizing that Mom's daily reminder to "Pay attention to detail!" wasn't just a work-ethic: It was a way of life. Mom lived attentive to the people, feelings, body language, sights, and stimuli around her. When she would describe her favorite places to me — places I had never been — she would tease my senses. Road tripping through California meant smelling the most divine flowery, citrus scent from the orange groves. Never has any scent been fresher than the cold water, clear air, and tart fir trees in Yosemite. The gelato shop in Positano smelled like baked sugar and berry-fruit. Adjectives and setting the stage. Attentive to detail. Attune to the magic.

The truth is that if we all paid, say, 30% (random percentage haha) more attention to any individual context or situation, then each of us would likely notice something that someone else doesn't. We are each created with our own distinctive awareness. Some of us are drawn to lines and symmetry and architecture. Some of us crave texture and pattern play (hang out with someone like this and you will realize how many patterns are everywhere!). Some relish trivia facts, history, or random general knowledge. Some can't ignore sounds and others smells and others "vibes." Some get numbers and logic, some filter everything through humor and irony, some make sense of things through fashion and shapes. Some like the colors and some see the shadows. Some grasp through theory and other through analogy. Some stillness and others action.

Pay attention, all of us!, to the details. I looked up definitions of magic and found it quite lovely that one source defined the informal use of magic as: "wonderful." The word is plain and poignant: wonder full. Just a great way to think of magic: something wonderful! Another source defined the descriptive use of "magic" as: any extraordinary influence as in "the magic of music," or "the magic of spring."

***

No surprise then, that my mother fell hard for the wonderful, influential magic of Disney. There seems to be two clear camps when it comes to Disney, those who either love or enjoy "all things Disney" and those who, um, don't. For the readers who are already obsessed, enjoy my mother's joy! And for the readers who are not, I hope what I describe to you helps you know my mom even better and maybe inspires you to enjoy whatever "magic" you do love in life. To be clear, this isn't a defense of Disney. I'm okay with not everyone enjoying the exact same things. Makes the world go 'round. I hear you: it's an expensive, over-rated, cafeteria-fed, sugar-rush-ing, kid-unhinging, stressful, scheduled, long-lined, too-hot, too-herd-like, too-fake, brilliant-marketed, nightmare of a way to spend your time. But not for my mom...or her mom...or for me.

Walt Disney was a man of his time, with flaws and some "blind spots" in his vision and character. For all the effort he put into excellence he dropped the ball at times and mishandled matters that impacted the lives and careers of people working with him. Walt battled a numbness of soul, that he acknowledged leading him to deep discouragement for most of his adult life. He was capable of bad, impulsive financial decisions that set his company back. He experienced both rejection and failure. But it's quite clear that he had a profound determination and ability.

He loved childhood and children, and he yearned for whatever that "thing" is that children have. He sought to bottle it up for everyone to drink. Walt's guiding principle? "Over at our place, we're sure of just one thing: everybody in the world was once a child. So in planning a new picture, we don't think of grown-ups, and we don't think of children, but just of that fine, clean, unspoiled spot down deep in every one of us that maybe the world has made us forget and that maybe our pictures can help recall."

Raised in a small town, with a simple, back-aching life — he knew the struggle and toil of his parents and the adults around him. He aspired to something different. That, in and of itself, is impressive. To step aside from the familiar flow of the stream and say "You know? I don't think this is for me." And it can change your life. He brought living, emoting, lovable, relatable little fellows to life with the prosaic tools of pencil and paper.

On a now famous train ride across the country (after a huge, potentially debilitating "no") a mouse was created, on tracks built by hard-working dreamers from generations before. Disney's breakthrough feature-length film,

Snow White, had the specific goal of evoking both laughter and tears. Disney believed and sought to demonstrate that story — even animated story — could both display humor and touch the heart, even in a deep place. Many have noted that Disney movies almost always include the loss of a parent or two, a partner, or a loved one (*Bambi, Snow White, Cinderella, Lion King, Aladdin, Tarzan,* etc, etc).

Disney was devotedly married to his bride, and they had a tender relationship. Their little girls were the apples of their eyes. And his grand idea of Disneyland arose from a Saturday morning with his daughters at a local park. They spun on a carousel as he sat on a bench waving and thought, "I wish there was a place designed for parents and children to have fun together." This creative, heavy-hearted, but hopeful father set out to bring to life the imaginary worlds of children. Worlds that had lived in the minds and hearts of young ones, through neighborhood play, the magic of books, and the mysteries of private story-telling. In his own words: "Every child is born blessed with a vivid imagination. But just as a muscle grows flabby with disuse, so the bright imagination of a child pales in later years if he ceases to exercise it."

Disneyland was designed to be a place where wonder, nostalgia, and togetherness were fertilized and watered. I know that this is not every visitor's experience, but I firmly believe if you want to fall in love with it, if you want to let it move you, if you try to reminisce and remember your favorite childhood sweetness, you can find the magic there too. My grandparents sure did. As newlyweds with their whole life ahead of them, they took a trip down the freeway to see what the fuss was all about in Anaheim. Despite Disneyland's epic opening day disaster (almost everything that could have gone wrong did), the company pressed on and corrected problems.

Within months of that day, Carol and Richard Kearney were wandering the colorful, balloon-filled, candy-scented streets of the magic land and they were hooked. They were there for the most "pure" form of the Disney vision, when Walt himself was likely somewhere in the park checking in on things. One of the very first vacations they took after their darling daughter was born was to this place made for families. I swear my grandparents' ability to tap into that inner-child spread like fairy dust to their kids. Don't you remember with fondness the times your parents were so happy? It does something in the heart of a child.

***

My quiet grandfather was sober-minded, emotionally-distant, and to this day his kids and grandkids smile to recall him tapping his foot and clapping his hands to the parade-music down Main Street. Even better, we laugh ourselves to tears remembering how he would just wander off from the group, to explore Disneyland on his own (Scrooge-type that he was!) and hours later we'd be walking and someone would spot Grandpa at the helm of the Mark Twain Riverboat — wearing mouse ears. He'd crouch his extra-long, bony legs onto a jeweled white horse, as he rode the merry-go-round alone. His usual frown was slightly upturned. It was real. Even he was happy there.

Since a trip is expensive for the average family, it took my parents a couple years to save up for our first visit. Mom had always talked about Disneyland, and we had little sing-a-long video cassettes we watched with un-blinking eyes. But I'll never forget the rosy cheeks and ecstatic energy the night Mom and Dad announced to us that we were going.

It was winter and they had been secretly planning a dream Christmas vacation with my grandparents and all my aunts, uncles, and cousins. Both Mom and Dad worked at the time, and they lived on a coupon-Goodwillpenny-pincher budget. Yet they had managed to accumulate enough (whether by generosity, saving, credit card points, or selling things) to fly all four of us kids and themselves from Maryland to California to spend the holiday in a wintery snow cabin with the extended family. And while we were there, we were going to Disney.

After dinner and baths one night they gathered us in the family room for "a talk." I was in first grade, so Timmy was probably five, Katie would have been three, and Kevin was a baby. They had a whiteboard set up on an easel that my dad borrowed from work. He used the dry erase markers from his coaching bag. We were probably much too young for it, but they had a 10-word hangman drawn up on the board. Since I was the only one who really knew what letters were, I guessed my way to being able to sound out "Diiizzzn-eh-l-ay-en-da." Mom and Dad simply glowed. Watching them, I almost expected the announcement to be that we were moving to a castle, because it turned out we are all kings and queens. But, I guess when you embrace Disney, you kind of are. "We're going to DISNEYLAND!" Mom helped and they tackled us and gathered us in their arms! "Can you BELIEVE IT!!" Mom shouted! It's funny because I sort of could believe it? I was six and knew nothing of money or costs, and I was extremely imaginative, so most anything seemed possible to me!

I remember my general feeling being "Huh, cool!" but my response did not match my parents, and that — more than anything — got my attention. Tucking us into bed that night, with more "We can't wait to take you!" and "Are you ready to finally be there?!'" I felt butterflies for the first time in my memory. I fell asleep to the orange hallway light turning my blankets purple and my parents doing dishes together with bubbly voices.

It was magic.

The whole Kearney clan — all 17 of us — three generations deep, parked in the original parking lot (before California Adventure, that sits there today, was built). We rode the tram (basically a large golf cart pulling a bunch of covered seats like a centipede) to the front gate. We were there early and it was still cloudy. All the girl-cousins had worn pink and teal foam curlers to bed, so we looked especially Shirley Temple in our red leggings and navy blue mouse sweatshirts. The excitement building between my aunts and grandparents surpassed birthday parties, special surprise outings, and even Christmas itself.

I don't think I actually remember the first moments of seeing the sea-foam green, iron ticket-queues, or hearing the lively murmur of fellow park-goers gathering. I don't think I remember the first time I heard the snort and cheerful "ring ring" of the perfect, red storybook-train chugging into equally darling Main Street station. I don't think I remember the enormous Mickey Mouse-shaped flower gardens, separating us from the train, or the old-style band music echoing through the pavilion. I was only six, after all, so I couldn't possibly remember the details of smelling ice cream, waffle cones, and warm, salty popcorn when rounding the first corner and the Olde Timers Waltz Melody being turned up louder. It doesn't matter. Every time I walk through that grey stone tunnel and see the plaque overhead declare: "Here you leave today, and enter the world of yesterday, tomorrow, and fantasy." I'm six years old all over again.

***

I understand money now. I understand that it comes only by hard, rump work. I understand that cells inside bodies error and start to destroy themselves and wind rips through homes and leaves them in splinters and horrible men crucify children and bullies walking the halls of every school make someone's 8:00 am to 3:00 pm a living terror. I've lost so much of that glory-eyed sense of innocence — the easy happiness I did indeed have as a child. I have lived long enough (in only 26 years) to watch my grandmother, both grandfathers, and mother do that thing that parents in Disney movies do: die.

"Life is composed of lights and shadows, and we would be untruthful, insincere, and saccharine if we tried to pretend there were no shadows. Most things are good, and they are the strongest things; but there are evil things too, and you are not doing a child a favor by trying to shield him from reality. The important thing is to teach a child that good can always triumph over evil, and that is what our pictures attempt to do."

–Walt Disney

Maybe Disney isn't the place that you choose to lose yourself and heal your heart and be filled with hope all over again. But it is mine. I understand, now, why my grandmother needed it. After seven years of miscarriages, and then losing her firstborn, after only a week and half with him in her arms. In a marriage maybe not be as vibrant and romantic as she thought it would be. After finding out (what we all do eventually): there are indeed evil and very sad things. And I understand, now, why Mom had shimmer shining through her cheeks when she could finally take her babies to a magic kingdom. I understand why Aunt Pam always cried during the fireworks, and why all the uncles carted strollers and bags and sleeping children around, waiting at ride exits nearly all day long.

It's not about pink and yellow Victorian buildings or Polynesian rainforests half-made (very realistically, I might add) in a factory or a fairy garden tour by row boat or the rootin' tootin' fiddlers in "the Wild West" or little girls in blue ball gowns meeting the "real" Cinderella. It's about hope. It's about believing good things ARE the strongest things. And they really do matter. It's about getting your sad, burdened, busy, lonely, rusty brain to connect the dots to something — anything — wonderful and truly be able to say, with all your self, "This is good. This is really good." Even if "this" is a bite of fried dough. Or, perhaps, a dream town come to life where parents and children can have fun together.

Just as Mom was facing the beginning of her final two years (almost to the day), I was able to take my dear boyfriend to Disney World for the first time. I genuinely had no idea he had a ring in his pocket all day. As Tinker Bell's fairy dust sparkled over the hidden speakers, alerting the crowds gathered at the foot of the castle that the fireworks show was about to begin — I was blissfully unaware that he was moments away from asking me a most magical question. The pops and sparkles in the sky, the castle lit up blue and purple, the "ooo's" and "aw's" of toddlers and hunched-over old men, the whistles, cheers, applause, the rising symphony soundtrack, a ring, and my dear love. I use cry-language with care: I mean it when I say I wept.

My dad says the best part of visiting Disney is walking up Main Street first thing in the morning and then walking back down it last thing at night. It's always the same. So full of bouncy, happy vigor upon arrival. Then, as you depart, it ushers you through a candle-lit, content dream; as though your heart has been tucked in with a kiss and the hallway light glows outside your cozily-dark room.

In the morning, mothers have their comfortable walking shoes tied tight, and everyone has that swollen, puffy "I'm up way too early" eye situation. There is indeed a pep in steps, and you'll find many hotel-shower-dampened heads. In the evening, close to the strike of midnight, sleeping children are bundled into strollers or tossed on their father's shoulders like bags of laundry. The music is slower. Folks wander out on throbbing feet and aching knees, and you'll find an assortment of families leaning on lamp posts and trash cans, waiting for Mom to grab "one last thing" from the Crystal Arcade. Everyone moseys.

We all hurt and are ready for crisp white sheets in a too-cold hotel room. It's magic.

And after dozens of these walks, one happy night, I added a piece of jewelry and a firm promise to that nighttime stroll. This time hand in hand with my even-better-than Prince Charming.

A year and a half later my mom held our firstborn son on his maiden voyage on her favorite "It's A Small World" boat ride. It was her first and last time visiting the park with our children. I'm grateful for the memory (more than anyone could ever know), but I can't visit now without being magnetically drawn to grandmothers there with their children's children. What a wonderful treasure. I sputter up with tears every time we arrive.

***

The magic finds me there and I can't escape the power of GOOD. It takes a hold of me and reminds me of the hope which I believe with all my heart — the promise of a real Magic Kingdom after this life, full of the Father and His children having fun and enjoying every pleasure, all together, forever. It is fitting that I began to miscarry our second child as I was sitting on a white chair on a pink patio during a Disney show. Caleb took me to the nurses' station and I was wheeled out of the park. Caleb and I spent the night at a Los Angeles hospital room. The contrast of my joy and my grief have never been more side by side. But I wouldn't have had it any other way. At Mom's memorial service we played a Main Street USA song loop, as over 1000 people entered the church to be seated and as they exited the auditorium to eat and mingle and look our family in the eye.

I think magic is anything that can influence you to remember what is good. And it is found everywhere. It is found in hospitals, in graveyards, across bodies of water, atop mountains, in trees, in museums framed from wood that came from trees, in outdated kitchens, on sidewalks, in fields, in minivans, on bleachers, under umbrellas, outside your town, and inside it too. Wonderful magic is in the sky and under the dirt, and it's living so easily in the hearts of children and in traffic jams and in the hairs of our skin that stand up from their lazy sleep when we really find it. Magic in word play, bedrooms, a paper bag containing something new, painted toenails, late night inspiration, wine with dinner, the feeling after you cry, the sound of a grocery cart in the spaghetti sauce aisle, when your ears pop, a toddler using the bathroom for the first time, and the moment you have the perfect, well-timed comeback.

Mom was attentive to these details, eager to let them wash over her and take her on their ride. I can say without hesitation that her discerning, watchful eye — that sought enchantment and knew its importance in the story — is what she planted in me before I was born. As she tended to my magic seeds and fingernails and bedroom sheets and vegetable intake and tears —she watered. When she stared at me as I was laughing, when she snuck into my room for one more forehead kiss when she thought I was asleep (but I wasn't yet), when she let me pick french fries out of the bottom of the bag, when she presented me before the throne of God in hundreds and thousands of prayers — she was my sunshine.

***

At the young age of fourteen I wasn't just an early romantic, I was blossoming through attentive care, hard work, and magic. Weddings mattered to me at a deep level; in a way I couldn't even put words to. I knew they mattered. I felt in my soul — beyond flowers and dinner arrangements and four-figure gowns — that this whole thing was significant. Quickly I found photography and it wasn't really about "art" or "expressing myself" or "documentation" at first. It was about hunting down magic. It was about believing with all my heart, even then, that the details and storylines that brought them to this day —and were this day — mattered. It filled me with wonder. Photography was a way for me to zero in, pay attention, and then show people what I found. As a favorite song goes: "Tell me everything that happened / Tell me everything you saw / They had lights inside their eyes / They had lights inside their eyes" (Dead Hearts by Stars).

Through photography I have explored the world, met many incredible people (including forming some of my dearest friendships), learned about music from nearly every decade, expanded my taste preferences, been in the room as multiple lives have entered the world, saved family memories for sometimes ten years in a row, and been challenged in business and customer care and finance and creativity and order. And its how I came across my husband. Photography has been, along with writing, a way for me to feel and a way for me to connect to my heart as well as to hearts around me. It has been the language I can use to show what I can't say. It's a showcase of extraordinary, in the ordinary. I'll live my whole life grateful for Mom sharing her magic findings with me, and for teaching me how to "treasure these things up in my heart."

I suppose if magic is anything "wonderful" or "any extraordinary influence" — Mom was magic herself.

What Mama Bear Taught Me About...
9. DEATH

"I'm standing on the seashore. A ship at my side spreads her white sails to the morning breeze and starts for the blue ocean. She's an object of beauty and strength and I stand and watch her until the sea and the sky come down to each other. And then I hear someone at my side saying, 'There, she's gone.' Gone where? Gone from my sight, that is all. See, just at the moment when someone at my side says, 'There, she's gone' there are other eyes watching her coming...and there are other voices taking up a glad shout, 'Look! Here she comes!'"
—Henry van Dyke

When Bacca, the name I used for my mom's mom, was diagnosed with breast cancer for the second time, my parents had already had their first four children. Four children in five years, no less. Dad was in the throes of "establishing a career" and Mom worked part-time as a nurse. Thanksgiving, 1997 my dad was offered a job that would relocate him from the Washington DC area to Southern California. Much of the decision to take the job was based on Bacca's health and my mom's desire to be near her. So we went on New Years Day, 1998, and spent 15 months living within a few hours of our lovely, determined grandmother.

During that time my parents were in serious discussions about their family size. It's their story to tell, so I won't go into too much detail; but my mom was "done" having kids and my dad was, in theory, perfectly fine with that. Despite that, they ended up (at least) realizing they weren't comfortable with any available ways to make their current family-size permanent. As this thoughtful dialogue progressed, a change of heart emerged: they weren't going to decide when they were done, and they were faith-filled to have another baby or two if God made it possible. Mom was almost 40 at this point and assumed such outcomes would be physically shutting down.

In California they found out Number Five was on the way! They were thrilled, so was Bacca, and the family celebrated in the stucco house on Mattin Circle with a palm tree in the backyard. But a few weeks later Mom realized she was in the middle of having her first miscarriage. My dad mourned the death like it was a child he had known for years. Mom was in a numb state of shock. They both wondered if their family really might be done after all. Maybe her body wouldn't be able to do this anymore. Maybe their gut instinct that "four completed us" was accurate. In the whirlwind of appointments, questioning, and crumpled parent hearts; Dad's new job — that had brought us to California — was not working out. The branch he had been sent to was failing and he was traveling back and forth from Maryland for business trips most of the month. The dreamy dream was becoming hazy and twisted.

***

By spring 1999 we were headed back to Maryland, every last one of us disappointed we had to leave; but our family-joy was renewed in Mom's new surprise pregnancy. Unexpectedly she was having another baby! After all that, everyone especially appreciated the thrill of waiting to meet another one of our own. He was due August 1, 1999. We moved into a friend's basement in May and finally to our own house, in the perfect neighborhood, during early June (just in time for Mom to set-up a Mother Goose nursery for her possibly-last munchkin). We were refreshed to see old friends, summer was a pleasure in our area (we spent most days at the local pool), and Dad's job seemed to settle in a good place. The chaos and even sadness of a few months ago had appeared to iron out.

On July 24th, one week before Mom's due date, as we were headed out to swim, Mom got a phone call from her sister. She locked herself in her room and after over an hour came out, red-eyed, to let us know we couldn't go to the pool today. I was terrified, though I didn't even know what to fear. I had never seen Mom do anything like this. She returned to her room and talked to my dad, her midwives, American Airlines, and her sister again. That night we packed. I was going to Reno, Nevada with Mom tomorrow. Bacca had been hospitalized and had taken a turn, in what had been her fairly uneventful cancer journey. It looked like she was in her final weeks or months.

The shock and suddenness was a jolt. Only weeks earlier she had been on a cruise with Grandpa and looked better than she had in years. After filling my little carry-on, roll bag with cotton tanks and shorts, I went to Mom in her room. She was packing newborn clothes and blankets and mentally preparing to have a baby without her husband and near her mom. At one point she pulled out a black, maternity dress — to perhaps wear to a place where people wear black. But she hung it back up in her closet, refusing to bring it. She was going to see her beloved mama, not to say good-bye to her. Not yet.

Mom and Dad had a plan: she would go now for a week, and if she had the baby there she would stay a bit longer to recover and Dad would fly out to be with her. If she hadn't had the baby, she would fly home and have the baby in Maryland, wait the required two weeks, and then go back to Reno. Either way it looked like this trip was going to be the first of multiple journeys, depending on how quickly Bacca declined over the following months.

We flew direct the next day, and were met at the airport by my charismatic Uncle Scott — Mom's baby brother. He is always good at cheering people up and naturally creates a sense of ease. We waited and waited and waited on some luggage that had accidentally been shuttled to the wrong baggage claim. Mom almost left the airport without it, she was so eager to see her mother. Eventually, we found the bags and rushed to the car. The hospital was close to the airport, but we had an awful, scrambling time finding the right parking garage to get into the building Bacca was in. After circling, u-turning, and re-routing a handful of times, we got to the right place. My nine-month-pregnant daughter-mother had waited as long as she could; she hadn't slept in a full day and had flown thousands of miles. She was ready to see her mom. The elevator ride was painfully long, and when the doors "ding-ed" open Mom was the first one out.

We were met with an odd scene. My mom's two sisters and her dad were standing in the hall so we could see their faces when the doors split. Aunt Pam shook her head, Aunt Lynda pursed her lips. Both had tears in their eyes. "I'm so sorry. I'm so, so sorry." While we were unloading in the parking lot, the Lord brought Bacca home. We missed her by four minutes. I'm not sure I'll ever understand why God couldn't have given Mom a few moments, a bit of a "heads-up," one last chance to see her alive. But He didn't. And, just like the scenes in ER dramas, the next few moments were urgent, wailing slow-motion. Mom collapsed and her sisters rushed to hold her up and make sure she didn't accidentally hurt the baby. I watched Mom bob and heave up and down, like a barge in stormy seas, in an awful, screaming weep. I was rushed away to sit in the waiting room while someone arranged for a ride for me.

***

Here was my very first encounter with death — well, other than Mom's miscarriage — and the shock of it was the worst part to begin with. The finality of it was the worst part to end with. Through the next couple of days, my almost-ten-year-old-self spent most of her time observing. I listened in on

hours of laughter as the kids of this extraordinary woman hashed out
memories together. I uncomfortably sat through hours of the adults I knew
best staring like lethargic animals in a cage. I watched grown-ups turn red in
sadness and I saw them reach for each other. They loved on me, too. It was
great grace to watch grief in such a safe way at such a young age. As the week
wrapped up, Mom decided to fly home and have her baby in Maryland. Thank
God Snyder children are stubborn.

Eleven days past his due date, Michael was handed to us. His delivery was
scary because he had been very breech, but the midwives were able to flip
him into the proper position. In the process his hand had gotten stuck over
his head. When Mom started pushing, the first thing my dad saw was a limp,
blue baby hand. Thankfully all was well and he was perfect. He was also the
greatest gift my mom could have had in the wake of her sudden loss. One of
the Psalms talks about God collecting our tears in a bottle. In this case, He
collected them on a baby. Mom would hold her dark-haired, almond-eyed, fat
baby boy and cry and cry. She wasn't able to walk through the good-bye
process, to come to terms with the pace of death, to do any "last things." Her
best friend had been snatched by surprise, but her surprise little boy was
soothing some of the sting.

***

She never 'got over' losing her mom. Though she had many great years and
memories left, there was always a piece of her that carried her sadness. The
loss had come so suddenly, and she never got to say good-bye. She
experienced emotional whiplash and her soreness never fully went away.
Since she didn't get to see her mom alive on that trip, she reflected on the last
time she did see her mother. What a story that is.

Bacca and Grandpa had booked flights for their cruise that happened to lay over in Baltimore. They were supposed to be there for three or four hours, so Bacca mentioned it to my mom. My mom didn't hesitate for a second. She was six months pregnant, after just moving to a new home, with four kids, and she drove over an hour to the airport — knowing she would probably spend close to two hours in rush-hour traffic on the way home from the airport. A willing price to spend a late lunch with her mom. We arrived at the airport a little early and watched the Arrivals screens for their flight. Quickly she saw their flight had been delayed. It was going to be an hour late. An hour passed and it still showed an hour late. Another hour passed, and the monitor still reported "DELAY." Almost three and half hours after their scheduled arrival, they landed.

Bacca and Grandpa rushed off the aircraft with only minutes to spare before boarding their next flight. Since this was pre-September 11, 2001, we were able to meet them at their gate. We power-walked through the airport, Mom almost jogging to keep up and Grandma being as present, doting, and sweet as ever. We sat at their gate for no more than two minutes before the airline employee announced Group A could begin to board. Bacca hugged us all, thanked Mom profusely for taking the time and going through all the trouble, and we waved good-bye as they disappeared down the ramp. That was the last time.

Thinking back on that story I've often thought, "Man, isn't it amazing Mom decided to go? What if she hadn't? She could have never known then that it would have been her last minutes with her mom on earth!" But the truth is: Mom would never, ever have passed that up. No matter what. It wasn't "by chance" that we were there in BWI — this was how Mom lived her life. She always parked and came in to airports if she was picking us up and always parked and came in if she was dropping us off (usually with the hopes of having a quick bite to eat together pre-security). And Mom was nearly always the one to pick me up. Even if the airport was a few hours away. If I was coming close to her, she was coming to get me. Caleb, who isn't a crier by any means, got misty a few months ago as we walked through the Orlando airport. "I just had a flashback to your mom waiting for us here in her colorful pants. I really miss her." It was never a burden for her to sacrifice anything to show up in the flesh, for her people.

And then the tides turned.

***

I've mentioned Mom being diagnosed with cancer numerous times throughout this account, but the "official" timeline is as follows:

In the winter 2002 Mom felt a lump in her left breast. A test was run and she was told it was definitely not cancer and that at some point she should get this benign mass removed, but there was no hurry. The following fall, about 9 months later, Mom gave birth to her seventh child, Lauren. She had been breastfeeding when she got pregnant; and was continuing to breastfeed her newborn, so she put a breast surgery procedure on hold until she was finished. The lump was still there, she noticed, but remained unconcerned about it.

In September 2003, almost a year later, Mom found out she was pregnant! She was about to turn 44 and really couldn't believe she was having another baby. However, her usual nausea symptoms did not set in like normal and she quickly suspected this baby was not going to live. Her instincts were correct and in November, 2003 she had a miscarriage that resulted in standard tests and procedures for someone in her age bracket — including a mammogram. This time the test revealed that the lump was cancerous and had been all along. It had been growing and spreading for the last year and a half.

In December, a few weeks after her diagnosis, she had a lumpectomy to remove the cancerous knot. During the operation doctors discovered the cancer had spread to her lymph nodes in her arm-pit region. A mastectomy was scheduled and done quickly. By the new year, she was starting a half dozen rigorous rounds of chemo, falling very sick each time (as told in detail previously). These treatments continued through the spring, and then in the summer immediate and intense radiation began.

As a new school year started, in what was now September 2004, we were elated to hear the news that after two surgeries, six chemo treatments, and 30 radiation treatments — preliminary tests said she was cancer-free. However, since cancer had access to her blood stream through her lymph nodes she would have to wait five years to be deemed "officially" in remission. I had turned 15 a month before the hopeful news, and Lauren was two months away from her second birthday. Fast forward the full five years (with check-ins every six months) and Mom was pronounced to be in full remission, with no evidence of cancer in her body!

***

One summer later, in 2010, the family moved to Florida for a work opportunity and, honestly, a change of scene for everyone. I stayed behind in Maryland, as I had just turned 21 and moved into a little apartment all my own. The Halloween weekend of that year I met Caleb. Around the holidays Mama's right arm started to swell far too much. She was diagnosed with lymphedema (localized fluid retention), most likely an after-effect of radiation. I flew down from Maryland to spend Christmas with my family in the Sunshine State, and Caleb made a dashing move by booking a ticket on Christmas Eve to fly that day to Florida to see me and meet my whole family.

Another year passed, and Caleb and I were ready to be engaged and start our life together. We convinced our families to spend Christmas together. His huge crew drove all the way from Oklahoma to Tampa, and my mom outdid herself trying to make a magical memory for us all. She was really busy, and had worked stunningly hard, but even so she was unnaturally weak and even struggled to breath.

Mom felt very guilty and bad that she had to rest so much. Regardless, she made magic happen on that trip: snowman pancakes with bacon scarves and chocolate chip buttons. A gingerbread house competition. A giant "welcome" banner made by hand. Handwritten glass table settings with everyone's name. Stockings for every single person. And hosting TWENTY NINE people in her average-sized house. We feasted every meal. She kept apologizing to me post-nap in her bed, confusedly saying, "I don't know why I'm so worn out!" I kept telling her, "Mom, you are going above and beyond. I don't think you realize! You should be tired!" But she knew it was more than just above-average sleepiness.

After everyone had returned home and school was back in swing, she took herself to a cardiologist wondering if something was wrong with her heart, to explain the difficulty breathing. The excellent doctor sent her to get a lung x-ray after finding nothing wrong with her heart, but agreed that her breathing was far too labored. She made this appointment for the first week of February in 2012. This x-ray revealed one completely collapsed lung and another lung filled with fluid like a water balloon.

She was scheduled for a surgery to try to re-inflate one lung, and drain the other. Right before Valentine's Day she was admitted to the hospital, and on February 15th I flew down to stay with her. After nearly two weeks in the hospital, dozens of procedures, and even more nasty meals — Mama came home. During her stay it was confirmed that her cancer was back in many places: breast, lungs, spinal cord, bones, liver, lymph nodes, and more. Her lung procedures weren't exactly successful (the one lung partially inflated and the other had drained only to begin slowly re-filling).

The doctors allowed her to go home, with strict orders on what to watch for should things turn sour. Caleb and I got engaged the weekend that Mom came home. We returned from Disney World at 3:00 am, and she was sitting in her pajamas and robe by the front door, with one lamp on, waiting to hug and celebrate with us. Within weeks her oncologist in Tampa began an aggressive chemotherapy plan.

Cancer has a numerical rating system. If you are cancer-free you will fall on the scale between zero and three. If you have a cancer number of 10, it is high. Mom's cancer number was 54. As sick as she had been the first time she did chemo, this was shockingly worse. But it was effective. By July her cancer number was all the way down to a five. Her doctor suggested she continue six more of the same treatment since it had worked so well. I was with Mom at this appointment and she almost cried at the doctor's suggestion. The woman who appeared to be able to handle anything felt like she simply could not do that form of chemo again for so long.

***

At this same time my family was packing up to move back to Maryland, and our wedding was six weeks away. In the middle of July, two moving trucks and three vehicles of Snyders drove up I-95 North, and on August 9, 2012 Caleb and I married each other and moved into the basement apartment in my parents' house.

Mom did two more of those chemo treatments, instead of six, and was still struggling to breathe well. Her oncologist in Maryland suggested she have a surgery done to try to get her lungs to "stick" back up to her interior chest wall. It was grueling and not particularly effective. She lost a lot of weight at this point and became "the sickest" and weakest we had ever seen her.

I was newly pregnant with our first baby, and I remember driving to Shady Grove Hospital (the same one where I would deliver our baby in a couple trimesters), and I was so sick I laid on the chair in Mom's room throwing up while she laid in her hospital bed throwing up. It was a bonding moment! After she had recovered from surgery she had a couple good months, which happened to be holiday season. She could drive, was regaining strength, and even cooked part of the Thanksgiving and Christmas meals. She went with me to many of my prenatal appointments, and she was in a content season of enjoying simple pleasures like eating and having hair. A PET scan taken in March 2013 showed that Mom's cancer was growing again, especially in her liver and bones. She started another new chemo — 12 treatments in 12 weeks.

In May 2013, when I was eight months pregnant and she 75% of the way through the current treatment, another PET scan revealed that the chemo wasn't working nearly enough. Her doctors fashioned a new plan of attack. Mom saw a specialist who recommended a brand new, particular chemo. This began immediately. In fact, Mom was at the Shady Grove Cancer Center for treatment the day I went into labor with Rowdy, so she went right from her appointment to the Labor & Delivery Unit. On June 14, 2013 Mom's first grandchild was born and she was there with Caleb and I for the whole 34 hour process of getting him out. I think Mom was hanging on to meet him.

As summer rolled into to fall, Mom unsuccessfully tried about four different chemo variations. All the PET scans said these medicines were not halting, ridding, or exterminating her cancer. In the middle of these treatments, at the end of August, we took that dream family vacation to California and Disneyland. Some of the best days of our lives. Mom looked radiant, healthy, and happy. Two months later, in October, Mom felt dizzy and jittery, and a brain scan was ordered. We found out the cancer had spread to her brain. Immediate brain radiation began, and chemo was halted for the time being. Radiation was by far the worst thing Mom ever went through. She was never the same after that. I remember many times walking into a room where she was napping and taking a deep breath before walking over to make sure she was breathing. This is when I came to grips with the reality that she was probably not going to get better.

In November we were happy to find out that the radiation had done some good work on her brain and that the cancer there was shrinking very well. The doctors felt it was important to jump back onto the chemotherapy train fast. We were told at this point that unless chemo began to work, she would only have months to live. I didn't find this too startling, but it was very sad, especially because only a couple months before we had heard that she probably had at least two years left during which she could likely manage the cancer. Christmas was sweet but hard.

Fifteen days after Christmas I took Mom to a very important PET scan. This was a big one. We needed to see some kind, any kind of positive elimination of cancer to have hope. Five days later my mom's best friend Tracy went with her to hear the results of the scan. I was at home with almost all the kids and saw Tracy pull into the drive way and very slowly help Mom out. Everything was grey outside. Mom struggled to make it up the stairs, even with help, to her bed. Tracy's eyes were red. Mom's eyes were tired. We popped our heads into her room like the forest critters in *Snow White* did upon discovering the girl in their woods.

"Come in," she told us. Dad finished a work call and joined us. I laid on her bed nursing Rowdy, who was seven months old, and Caleb leaned his head on my arm. Katie lay on her stomach next to Mom, and held her hand. Shannon and

Lauren kneeled at the edge of the bed. Dad stood in the corner, pacing. Michael stood, as well. Kevin hadn't come home from school yet but would be there shortly. We were quiet, waiting for what was obvious but awful.

"Well," Mom said, "I have some good news and I have some bad news. The good news is that I don't have to do chemo ever again…" My eyes quietly filled up with salty, sad water. "The bad news is…that I'm dying," she said calmly. Katie scooted her whole body closer and dropped her head into the blankets. Shannon and Lauren looked confused as they started to cry. Dude rubbed his tongue along the inside of his mouth, and the lump in his throat was almost visible. Kevin loudly banged in the front door and stomped up the stairs, flinging her bedroom door open, finding us all in tears. "What did they say?!" he innocently asked. Mom nodded her head and said "It's time for me to go Home." Kevin fell to the wood floor so hard it sounded like he had cracked his head open. Mom, who could hardly lift her arm without help, flew into a sitting position and screamed, "Is he okay?! Somebody help him!!" Kevin moaned and shook in full-soul grief while Caleb and Dad tried to help him up. It was the worst.

***

My memory becomes a bit of a blur for the rest of that day. We stayed in her room most of the night, and at one point she and I talked realities. "How much time did they say?" I asked. "She said 'weeks' but I don't know if that means two weeks or six weeks," Mom answered. "I wonder if you'll be able to watch us or 'be with us'…" I wondered. "I know! I hope I'll be able to! I've always assumed I will…But who knows how it works?" she said. "If there is a way for you to be near in real time, can you let us know through pink?" I asked. "Pink?" "Yes," I elaborated, "like, pink flowers or pink skies or pink anything." "I can do that," Mom promised. She told me she was ready. She didn't want to leave us, because she knew it would make our lives hard and sad; but she said she was worn out and ready.

We made a list of things to do before she went. We were going to borrow a cap and gown so Dad, Mom, and Kevin could take graduation pictures together. We scheduled a wedding dress fitting at a posh boutique downtown so Katie could try on gowns with Mom. Tim was going to take Mom on her last date. We were looking into dinner cruises on the Potomac River to be a small stand-in for the Caribbean Cruise Mom was supposed to take the youngest three on. Before Bacca died she had plans to take the whole family: kids, spouses, and grandchildren on a giant family cruise for their 45th wedding anniversary. She died before making it to that milestone, but our grandfather still gave his kids the money to take all the grandkids. They just did it in three separate trips: the oldest cousins went together, then a couple years later the middle cousins went, then the youngest cousins were supposed to go together. But Mom was going to miss this last one.

We set a date for an "open house" where friends and loved ones could come to the house, pray, worship, and encourage Mom. A true good-bye party. Hospice arrangements were made. Four days after the final appointment, all the girls went to Georgetown to watch Katie try on dresses she could never afford, and Mom beamed. One "to do" down.

***

The day after wedding dress shopping, Rowdy woke up from an afternoon nap very hot. I took his temperature and it was 100. Thirty minutes later I took it and it was 101.5. I called the pediatrician and explained that he seemed completely normal before his nap, but seemed floppy, lethargic, and "off" now. She had us come in and when we arrived his fever was 104.5. She turned us right around and sent us to the emergency room. While we were there he seemed a bit more himself and his fever went down to 103. I thought they would give us some medicine and send us on our way. After six hours, however, the doctor informed us that Rowdy had a kidney infection and that they were going to admit him until his fever was gone for more than 24 hours and the infection cleared. I was so taken aback.

We went up to the children's floor and set him in the giant, metal, cage-looking bed to sleep. He was hooked up to IV's for medication, and every time he'd settle down and get into a deep sleep, it was time for another round of vitals. Caleb and I shared one chair and slept together in sporadic bits. Rowdy's fever continued rising and dropping, rising and dropping. When the morning doctor arrived she wanted to have an ultrasound done on his kidneys.

After lunch we were wheeled through the hospital to a tech. She was pleasant but reserved and chatted lightly with us. All of a sudden, though, I could see her working a little faster. She stopped talking, and stayed on the same spot taking pictures over and over. She adjusted slightly to get other angles. I, fully untrained, couldn't tell from the screen what she was looking at, but I — very used to medical bedside manner — knew she had found something that was concerning her. Without addressing us she stood up and left the room, not making eye contact. "She saw something," I quivered to Caleb.

Our transport came back into the room and returned us to our floor. Rowdy fell asleep in the crib, and I emotionally unraveled. It would be a few hours before we got to speak with the doctor about the results. I knew she had seen something. "I think Rowdy has tumors in his kidneys, Caleb." "Kristen. Stop. Don't let your mind wander. We just need to wait and see. Worrying won't help anything." I couldn't stop. The weight of the world knocked me over like a too-tall block tower. My son is sick, I'm going to lose my mom and my son at the same time, This is going to do me in, I'm going to die too, Caleb is going to be left alone which will probably break his heart, I can't do this... I've never felt my heart race so quickly, and I struggled not to hyperventilate. I couldn't hold a cup of water or fork still because my hands were shaking with so much fear and adrenaline.

Though it was only two hours, it felt like days that we waited for the doctor. Immediately, I was put at ease by her casual entrance and light-hearted facial expression. "Alright, Mom and Dad, these scans look good. The only thing I'm taking a look at here is a funny shaped hook at the bottom of his kidney," she pointed out. "Usually kidneys are shaped like this" she held her fingers up in a U-shape, "but his look more like this" she bent her index finger. "I don't see anything wrong, though! Sometimes things are shaped a bit differently and that's okay. Everything appears to be working just right and I have no concerns." I could have squeezed her so tight her kidneys popped.

***

I can't even compare thinking for two hours that your kid might be sick with actually finding out your child is sick, or 1000 times worse, is going to die. This incident was the closest my mind had come to imagining such horror, and I felt like I got a whiff of the lung-sucking distress a parent would feel. I don't have words. I had never before and I have never to this day gone to as dark and terrified a place as I did for those two hours. I simply cannot fathom what such loss would be like, and I have no greater respect or empathy than for parents who have known such a situation as their real life, not just an idea (starting with my husband's parents, who lost their three-year-old son, Joel, and my dear Castro friends, who live without their little girl, Alivia).

We stayed a second night at the hospital, waiting for the fever to stay clear. We were on track to go home the following afternoon as his first normal temperature had been taken around noon. We woke up Saturday morning,

January 18 — the day the boy's Varsity team was scheduled to play a home game against a long-time rival. In light of the news regarding Coach's wife, the school was having a Pink-Out for Mama Bear. A friend offered to stay at the hospital with Rowdy so Caleb and I could go. We were worn out, frumpy, and wrinkled; but we went to the game and helped keep score — so blessed by the many fans who came out and wore pink shirts. Mom was in the corner, like always, sitting in her wheelchair and hooked up to her oxygen tank. We felt flooded with love and support by our community. And the boys took home a nice big win to seal the sweetness of the day. Caleb and I returned to the hospital where we found out that a mistake had been made: Rowdy never had a kidney infection, just a bad winter bug; but his fever was gone and we could go. I was too tired and relieved to ask many questions, so we packed fast and we fled home.

I laid in our king-sized bed just taking deep, grateful breaths as I thought about taking a real nap for the first time in a few days. As I closed my eyes, my sister Shannon started calling my name. "Mom needs help, Kristen!" It wasn't that I had forgotten about Mom, but I had certainly become preoccupied enough with my boy to have it feel like a snap back to my other reality: my dying mother. I jumped up and spent the rest of the day in her room. Aunt Pam had flown in that day, as well. It was happy to have her with us.

Sunday, January 19, was a quietly peaceful day. Mom told me that she could feel her mom nearby and that she was very, very tired. We worked together to make sure the kids would have letters from her for future special days in their lives that she would miss. We all slept well and Monday morning was bright but chilly. We asked Mom what she wanted for breakfast and she said, "nothing." This wasn't strange, but then she didn't want anything for lunch either. I felt a little nervous, but I knew that she would let us know when she felt able enough to put food in. This is when I made her a spread of food on a plate and set it on her night stand. Rowdy, Aunt Pam, and I were in the bedroom with Mom and I was showing her pictures of our time at the hospital. She made sad faces seeing her precious grand-boy, in a little green gown, connected to cords. "Poor baby!" she commiserated. She started to get sleepy and without warning was napping. This was also normal. She dozed in and out of sleep often. Aunt Pam read and I went and nursed Rowdy. Less than an hour later Mom woke up and was panicked. She wanted me to call her church friend, Charlene, who was also a hospice nurse. I ran, shaky, down the stairs to tell Dad. "Mom wants us to call hospice." We both knew Mom didn't make requests like this unless she needed them. It was happening. No no no no. Not yet. We didn't get everything done. There is an open house. It hasn't even been a week! We were going to have weeks! What happened! Dad cussed when he stood up to find his phone. Death deserves a cuss.

***

A couple hours later Charlene came to see how Mom was doing (she was with another patient or else she would have come immediately). The sun was beginning to go down as she assessed Mom. After spending some time with her, Charlene asked to speak with me privately. We sat down in the dining room together. "Okay, Kristen. I am here to help you and to support you in taking care of your mom. I will do everything I can to educate you and do what your family wishes during this time. You see, nothing is for sure, but in the hospice world we have three categories of time: weeks to months, days to weeks, and hours to days. The last time I saw your mom I would have said she was in the 'weeks to months' stage, but unfortunately there has been a change and I would say she is in her last hours to days. Now, I don't know if it will be three hours or three days, but it won't be much longer. Do you understand?" I did understand, and I sat there trying very hard to figure out how to be a big, brave, but broken-hearted girl.

The next few hours to days were not going to be easy. Charlene gave me some more information and suggestions, and we were going to go ahead and get her a first dose of morphine to help her be very comfortable. I felt sick to my stomach as I went back upstairs. Mom had been moved a little earlier from her bed to my dad's recliner. It was easier for her to breath sitting upright. I could hear her short, gargly breaths as I neared her room. When I came in and put my hand on her shoulder she opened her eyes right away. It was the first time in my life I'd ever seen her look small and scared. She looked up at me like I know I looked up to her when I needed reassurance and comfort. "What did Charlene say?" she whispered. My heart bled and my eyes stung as I willed tears not to enter them. "You're about to die, Mom, it's happening. I hate this so much and I'm so scared and I would do anything to stop this, please make it go away, Mom!" — is what I thought. "We're going to give you some medicine so you'll be very comfortable. It will help your breathing. You're just fine, we're going to take good care of you." — is what I said. I felt so protective of her. I wanted to shield her from as much as I could. She closed her eyes and I told her I loved her. She said "I love you." and fell asleep. This would be the last words she spoke on this earth. Beautifully enough, they were the first words she spoke to me on earth.

I told Dad and Aunt Pam what Charlene had told me, and we gathered all the kids up to her room. Telling them was heart-wrenching. I wanted to protect each one of them from this pain. We gathered around Mom in her chair, and held her hands, toes, and face in our palms. Worn out from pain, most of us fell asleep around her. The sun came up the next morning, Tuesday, the 21st, and Charlene stopped by to check on us all. We were all fast asleep and the house was peaceful. Charlene told me she wanted to make sure the coming hours were as calm and gentle as these were. She also mentioned the option of not giving Mom a dose of morphine this morning because there would be a chance we could communicate with her to say our good-byes while she was cognizant. "It would be extremely unlikely that she would open her eyes and talk at this point, but you might be able to communicate enough to tell her something she can hear and ask her to squeeze or tap your hand if she does." We decided it would be worth a shot to get to have her aware for our good-byes, as long as she wasn't miserable. If she started to seem in pain or upset, we would give her the medication right away.

I still don't think it was a bad decision to try to have "one last moment" with her. Heartbreakingly, however, it backfired a bit. Not giving Mom the medicine made her just aware enough to realize she was dying, but left her still drowsy and weak enough to not be able to communicate at all. She kept trying to arrange herself in the chair, but would get stuck and we could tell she was hurting herself. Caleb and Timmy carried her from the recliner to a hospital bed set up in the large room over the garage, with the hopes of helping her relax. She didn't. She knew what was happening and every last bit of her strong will, determination, and unearthly strength came out. She clenched her mouth shut, refusing to let us give her the medicine. She almost 'wrestled' us when we tried to prop pillows up for her head, so her neck wouldn't be craned. It was deeply horrible to watch her writhe and fight as she was. It was as if she was simply refusing her fate. My soul was in turmoil. I wanted to cry and beg her to stop. "Please Mom! Don't do this! It's okay! Please take your medicine! Please, stop trying to be so strong!" She had been so elegant, so sure, so ready to go. I felt flustered and anguished for her. What was wrong? What could I do?

Sovereignly, one of my mom's best friends texted me a couple hours into this hard afternoon. "Hey Kristen, I don't know if your mom told you, but when I came over a few days ago she had me write down all the important information for the kids. Their doctor's offices, where the important documents are, and things like that. It's in a black folder next to her side of the bed." I jumped out and ran over to the spot, and easily found the folder. Inside it was indeed all those "important Mom things" you tell someone who is going to watch your kids when you leave, especially if you will be gone forever. While she and I had made sure the kids had letters, she was going to write mine on her own. Inside the black folder was the first paragraph of an unfinished letter to me. It had a single tear stain on it. "Dearest Kristen, I have loved you with my whole heart since the moment I met you. I am so grateful I was able to be your mom. You are an amazing woman, and I am so proud of who you are. You're a wonderful wife and Mom. It was a highlight of my life to be with you while you had your first baby. I will be cheering you on from Heaven when you have more. I'm going to miss you." There was 3/4 of blank page left. "Oh Mom," I realized, "you are worried about us."

I literally ran back to her bed side. "Mom," I whispered as she was still tense and struggling. "I found the binder. I have all the information the kids need for healthcare and school and documents. I will make sure they are taken care of. And I found your letter. I'm going to miss you so much, too. I really am. But it's okay. We'll be okay. You don't have to take care of us anymore. It's okay, Mom. It's okay." I rubbed her bald head with my fingertips and cried. She immediately settled down. Her jaw relaxed and she finally dropped into her pillows and was still. Minutes later she let us give her more morphine, and she was in deep, comfortable, peaceful sleep once again.

***

The rest of the day we all rotated time in the room. We turned on *Saving Mr. Banks*, a Disney movie about Mary Poppins she had wanted to see but hadn't yet. We sang worship songs almost constantly. I read her emails and messages that were coming in online. There were so many people praying and carrying us. Darkness came once again and all was calm. The wind howled outside, the snow was thick in our yard. Katie crawled into bed with her and held Mom all night long. She was so brave. Death looks, sounds, and smells terrible; but Katie was not intimidated. She stared it right in the face and came close. I was so impressed and proud of her. Shannon and Lauren spent the night with good friends who gave them a bit of respite in this intense time. Aunt Pam and Charlene sat awake with Mom until the sun came back up. I was surprised we had come to another day with her still with us.

I crawled out of bed with my baby, and sat next to Mom. She looked worse. Much worse. Charlene told me it was close. I went to the bathroom and when I returned, I paused at the sight: the beautiful slanted-ceiling room, the one where my mom helped me put on my wedding dress, the one where we took newborn portraits a few months ago. The brightest morning sun was shining into the windows. My sleeping husband was on the couch, my sleeping brothers were on the floor, my sleeping sister hugging my sleeping mom, my loyal aunt and our godsend hospice nurse sitting at her feet. And I also could have sworn I could see angels sprawled about the room, too. I know I couldn't see it physically, but in my memory it's so clear I could draw out for you where golden heavenly beings sat on their knees or perched on couch arms. I could also "see" an intense whiteness in the upper right hand corner of the room. It reminded me of when you go outside without sunglasses on after being in a dimly lit room indoors. It felt like a porthole, like the door to Heaven was right there. I sat next to Mom and laid Rowdy in bed with her. He patted her face and stared quietly.

There was a build in adrenaline as the minutes passed, and it felt as if we were literally walking beside someone. Maybe like a father walking the bride down the aisle, only to pass her off once there. Everything felt close. Heaven, earth, healing, death, God, people. "I Will Rise" by Chris Tomlin come on the iTunes shuffle. A distinct change in breathing patterns occurred. We studied her chest as it began to slow down. "I think we have a few more minutes," Charlene told me. I reported to the rest of the family, in case they wanted to see her one more time. When I came back, the chorus of the song was playing. "Jesus has overcome / And the grave is overwhelmed / The victory is won /

He is risen from the dead." Mom breathed short and awfully slow. We watched. One second. Two seconds. Three seconds. Four seconds. Five seconds. Another very short, very slow breath with a slight rise of her chest. "I will rise when He calls my name / No more sorrow, no more pain." One second. Two seconds. Three seconds. "I will rise on eagles' wings / Before my God fall on my knees / And rise. I will rise." Four seconds. Five seconds. Six seconds. Seven seconds. "And I hear the voice of many angels sing, 'Worthy is the Lamb!'" Eight seconds. Nine seconds. Charlene got up from her seat and leaned close to Mom. Ten seconds. "And I hear the cry of every longing heart, 'Worthy is the Lamb!'" Her chest did not rise. Charlene checked her pulse then nodded, with tears in her eyes, "She's home." "Worthy is the Lamb!"

***

I can't explain the extraordinary, surprising joy that overcame me in those seconds. I had been quite nervous anticipating that precise moment, but when it came I felt celebratory. I felt like I was outside the door of a roaring stadium. As if the vibrations from the dancing and shouting were causing that bedroom to tremble. I felt *this* close and exceedingly happy for Mom. She was home! The body before my eyes was empty of her. She felt so alive to me in that moment — so healed, so whole. It felt more like she had just been born. Witnessing the exact moment of passing from here to there changed me at a core level. For the rest of my life I will be overwhelmingly grateful for the opportunity I had to walk my mother home. To watch her selfless, Mama Bear heart care more about us than herself until the true end. To be mesmerized by her beauty. To share in her suffering and in her joy. After the fact, I've realized how blessed we were to have such a good good-bye. To be able to be there, in the flesh, for my person after all the thousands of times she had been there for me. I do not take for granted the gift of watching her live and then watching her die.

***

Before noon, I had started sorting through the thousands of pictures we had of Mom or that were taken by Mom. I spent nearly every hour, day and night, after she passed, working on the video to show at the church. I went into a trance, only stopping to feed my baby. The morning of her service I woke up, after only three hours of sleep, before the sun. I never do that. I got dressed and came upstairs. I never do that. I found my dad drinking coffee and thinking alone in the living room. He does that every morning, always while it's still dark out. We looked at each other, took deep breaths, and lifted our eyebrows in that "Wow, what a few days" sad way. Seconds later, pink stripes unrolled across the wood floors and walls. We turned and looked out the front windows and saw one thing: pink. No trees or houses or cars. Just pink. I grabbed my phone and my sister's boots and ran through the foot of snow. Pink was everywhere. I spoke out loud: "MOM! I miss you! Oh Mom, thank you! I miss you!" The earth was dyed an unmistakable, electric, heavenly shade of pink. Since the white snow covered the ground, it soaked in the color of the sky fabulously. Pink bounced off every reflective surface — the windows and car mirrors and shiny mailboxes! Full 360 degree surround PINK. In 13 years of rising before dawn at that house and 32 years of living in that state and 56 years of being alive, my dad had never seen anything like it. I certainly had not myself. I think Mom opened the window to her new bedroom, in the new house her Father had prepared for her, and He let the light fall onto earth for a bit. He gave us eyes to see the supernatural for sixty seconds before it faded away into into grey-ish blue. She was still taking care of us, letting us know that she was there.

What Mama Bear Taught Me About…
10. BIRTH

"It was enchanting to meet you."
— Taylor Swift

"One of the saddest parts for me is knowing that I'll never get to give birth again," Mom shared with me early in her first cancer journey. The miscarriage leading to the discovery of her cancer was behind her and a new future with doctor-ordered barrenness was ahead. Given her age, the drugs she would be on, and the invasive surgeries, "giving birth" was a season of life now closed to her. Losing her hair was weird and not her preference, but she wasn't too bothered by it. She faced all her procedures with a game face and an educated, strong mind. She never once complained about being sick. She wanted to live longer and was willing to endure the battle for life.

The parts that were "suffering" to her were mostly centered around us: she wasn't allowed to be near the littlest kids and their germs very often. She was confined to bed and missed events more than she would have ever chosen. She worried about us if her life was taken by this disease. And she was done having babies. She didn't get to choose, it was chosen for her. It was a bit startling to go from "pregnant" to "never having any more children" in a matter of days. These were the issues that hurt her heart.

When she was in high school her dream was to go to a Christian college, marry a student two years her senior, and transition right to stay-at-home mom life. She knew she'd love being a mom and couldn't wait to dive in. When "the plan" took a dozen years longer than anticipated, she had learned a bit about cherishing. The woman cherished the chance to actually be a mother after years of wondering if it might not ever happen for her. She looked forward to participating in every bit of it. The discomforts and side-effects of pregnancy and delivery were willingly accepted (as part of a recovered hope) by a grateful woman. "Birth is not only about making babies. Birth is about making mothers." (Barbara Katz Rothman)

Mom had an especial grace given to her when it came to appreciating life. I look back and wonder, "Why? Where did she get that from?" My answers to this question are a casserole of God-given sensitivity, a great maternal relationship on earth, being a special-needs pediatric nurse, and having to wait.

And, before I continue much further, she would never want her love for giving birth to come across like some "natural birth guilt trip." Mom never looked down in tone or thought to women who neither wanted nor could have the birth experiences she did. For her it didn't have much to do with other women at all. It was simply how God wired her, and what instinctually was most appealing to her heart. She wanted the whole kit and caboodle. She wanted it all, she didn't want to be numb to any of it. And she believed it was best for us, her longed-for little babies. It was never a badge of honor or something she felt like she had to prove as a woman. If she were to sit down around a table of food and ladies asking her questions about childbirth, she would simply want to share a glowing, positive, empowering vision of a magical part of her life — with zero emphasis on the approaches of others being inferior to hers. The concept that a baby is in your body and then, somehow, comes out — however that might be! — blew her mind and captivated her.

With that caveat, you have to know this about my mom: she became nearly addicted to childbirth. Gary Allan Taylor says, "There is a Celtic axiom declaring heaven and earth to be but three feet apart, but in the 'thin places', that distance is even smaller. These 'thin places' exist where the veil separating heaven and earth is pulled back, revealing the glory of God. Sitting there, you reach out your hand and expect to feel Him, it's that palpable. And these are not simply places where God's presence is felt, but hallowed ground where heaven and earth are one, giving us a tiny glimpse of God's kingdom, regenerating creation all around us."

I've heard the sentiment, many times, that this veil is thinnest and, in fact, almost disappears, during birth. These feelings were Mom's exact experiences. For her there was nothing in her life to compare with the sudden, instant change from severity to relief, and the nearness she felt to every big, good thing in heaven and on earth during childbirth. I would ask her a hundred questions, and this topic was one where she would simply lose herself. I could see a physical alteration in her face and the gaze of her eyes, and she would recount to me the details of effort, smells, adrenaline, hunger, pride, and wonder. "It's not something you can just sign up to do, like sky diving. It's so specific and so big and not everyone gets to do it. And even once you've done it, you never know if you will get to do it again." She marveled at birth. My dad said that "birth is awe-inspiring, and she loved to be in awe."

***

"For as soon as Zion was in labor she brought forth you, her children... You shall nurse, you shall be carried upon her hip, and bounced upon her knees. As one whom his mother comforts, so I will comfort you." (Isaiah 66:8 and 12) The spiritual parallels she drew from the process of birth were foundational to the faith my mother possessed. They are also some of my favorite facets of my faith today.

For example, Mom found great honor in being allowed to carry each of us inside her very self. Isaiah 46:4 says, "I have made you and I will carry you." Her serenity grew with each child. Each time she had that positive test, she waited a couple of days to tell my dad. "I liked having a secret, just me and God. I liked being the only one in the world who knew about the life I was carrying inside me. It was special," she confessed. You could see how much she enjoyed being our cargo ship, and it's not because she had easy pregnancies. Just the opposite, in fact. As I've made clear previously: she was extremely sick for all of her pregnancies. When I was wobbling through my early weeks of shock-and-horror during Rowdy's pregnancy she encouraged me, "Just wait until you can feel that baby move. Feeling that little person will give you a lot of strength. You can do it." She did indeed consider herself a vessel being used to transport precious treasure from heaven to earth, and she was grateful for the privilege.

The anticipation of waiting for labor to start was another spiritual highlight for her. She likened it to Jesus' return — no one knows the day or the hour except for Him. She loved not knowing when it would all begin. Her babies liked to stay inside, and she carried the seven of us a grand total of sixty days past due. While we were waiting for Lauren to make her grand entrance, I was 14; and, frankly, I couldn't stand it! "Just go get induced! Don't you want her to come?!" I'd bemoan!

Mom was in no hurry. She knew nothing was wrong. There was nothing to force or make happen. And unless there was cause for alarm, her job was to carry on and look forward. When seasons changed, she would be ready. As long as everyone was healthy, she loved getting to "let God" choose the birth day; let her and the baby's bodies do what they were made to do.

The science lover that she was made her fascinate over the fact that scientists don't know exactly what starts labor. Yes, a hormone called oxytocin releases from the baby into the mother. But why does it release? She loved that scientific-research still hasn't figured this out; that it remains a mystery from heaven. "It's like God just whispers a thought into the baby's mind, 'Okay. It's time!'" she theorized. She also loved the preparations in her home. She was no award-winning home-cleaner, but when it came to decorating a room, she was magic. Not all of her babies had their own nursery, but some did. And she ("Without the internet! Or Pinterest, mind you!") would come up with such darling, affordable, time-consuming ideas to make us our own spaces — even if that was just a corner of her own bedroom. "I go to prepare a place for you." (John 14:3) These spaces were her love-language and part of her experiencing all the anticipation possible. The skill of expectancy was hers. She knew how to eagerly await.

Then, there was labor itself. Being that she was a short, blonde girl from California who grew up in middle-class America, it might be strange to find out that she was the "absolute toughest, bravest person" my dad has ever met. And he came from a rougher part of the world. "She had an ability to endure and face pain in a way I've never seen before or since." he told me. When he talks about what happened during all of our births, his mouth loosens and he shakes his head back and forth: "I can't explain it. I wish you could have seen her for yourself."

Mom said that labor starts out "unpleasant" and moves to a place that is "intense." "But," she'd reassure, "once you are at the worst place, it means you're almost done. It doesn't last much longer." She had a trick for herself: she thought she could handle anything for 10 seconds. Once contractions started to get so bad that she believed, "I cannot do this anymore." she would count to ten. "Usually the worst pain was over by then! And if not, I knew I could at least do it for ten more seconds."

She loved letting every other thought — the rest of the world — completely vanish while she got to disappear into the Land of Labor. There was nothing else to think about or care about. It was all-encompassing by force, and she appreciated the magnitude of such an experience. She told me "There are many things in life that are easy to get distracted from, and you have to work at putting your mind to focusing. But birth isn't like that. You don't get distracted thinking about when the phone bill is due." My grandma described birth as "all the power in the universe being funneled through your body." Mom didn't like pain, but she loved the ability to push through it and overcome. It made her feel close to God and to her child. "We remember before our Father your labor prompted by love, and your endurance inspired by hope in our Lord Jesus Christ." (1 Thessalonians 1:3)

And then, the moment. The veil-torn, in the flesh, no-longer-separated moment. Parent and child united, the smaller burrowing into the bosom of the larger. Together, at last. Of course, you've been together this whole time. But not like this. Not with unveiled faces. And this is just the beginning of a long, happy ending. If you've had children, you know how The Moment lives with you. Anita Diamant writes "There should be a song for women to sing at this moment, or a prayer to recite. But perhaps there is none because there are no words strong enough to name the moment." Science has found in recent years that the first hour after birth is critical — even calling it "The Golden Hour."

The physical, measurable, trackable effects of the mother and child bonding in those initial moments are changing hospital protocol across the world. Where standard procedure was to cut the cord and whisk the baby off for measurements, shots, cleaning up, and the like — there is a wave of change saying "No, it's best for mom to have her baby." Even for c-sections, doctors are making a steady change in the way post-delivery is handled and the changes are centered around basking in the glory for maximum bonding. How neat is that?!

***

After so many years of trying to understand and absorb the wonder of what Mom was describing, I had my own chance to give birth. Rowdy Neil Morris came into the world eight days past his due date, with copper hair, hilariously long limbs, and ready to sleep (hallelujah!). I labored at the hospital for 34 hours and ended up using pitocin (a labor-starter that increases the severity of contractions), while struggling through back labor (supposedly the most painful type of labor). One of the specific memories I have of that experience in my life was looking over at my mom, almost glaring, and saying "You lied to me." I did not feel close to heaven. This did not feel like "uncomfortable pressure." It felt so far past "intense" that it was laughable. It was the most exhausting, painful, never-ending, stuck, miserable thing. I could tell Mom felt bad for me. My dad has made it very clear that I am not like my mom in labor ("Thanks, Dad!"). But it's true: there has never been a time that I've been more aware of the strength of that woman. Like, whoa.

Wonderfully enough, when Rowdy left my body, we both reached for each other, he was laid on top of me, and a switch flipped. Almost instantly I was overcome with that euphoric relief Mom had talked about so often. Mom hadn't been lying. The extreme contrast of pain and sweet, sweet "God bless you, I'm never doing that again" sweet respite was other-worldly. I've never read the perfect description of a warm, wet baby being given to you, but it's not for lack of writers and mothers trying.

The soft, wet, lump of person is frantic and mad while trying to find that dark, safe, place he had so enjoyed for months. He starts to settle inside my palms, velvet baby ear pressed above my heart. His feet gently twitch on my rib cage, under the warm blankets with which we are covered. Caleb kisses my forehead and gasps and murmurs by my side. Mom looks so happy it appears her head might pop off. My friends are wiping tears from their eyes and they are breathy. Hormones are shooting off like fireworks of happiness. It feels...

like heaven. "I could live for the rest of my life on what we experienced that day." Sarah Bessey says well.

I hoped giving birth would be good, I thought it would be good, but it was better than I had the capacity to desire. Hands-down one of the most significant gifts of that day was my mom's support, prayers, help, wisdom, and happiness. I dreaded doing it without her.

***

A month after Mom passed away I found out I was pregnant again. Our little Ryan Day ("Child of The King") moved from life in my body to life in heaven three months later. His short existence on earth was the "straw that broke the camel's back" emotionally. My soul grieved, but believed that hopeful, happier days were ahead. They were. And just after Rowdy's second birthday — the day after Caleb decided to change careers and be a full-time musician — I found out there was another 'somebody' in there.

Within a few months I would know she was our daughter. My cheeks hurt from smiling the day we discovered "she was a she." I know many women want to have a daughter of their own, me included, but the longing intensified after losing my mother-daughter relationship on earth. I felt parched to have such a treasure again. I love having a little boy, and I would take half a dozen more of them, but knowing there was her began to heal some parts of my heart. I was and am grateful.

Mom always delivered us at a birth center run by midwives about twenty minutes from our childhood home. However, the practice has since shut down because of financial reasons. There aren't many midwife-run, out-of-hospital birth centers in Maryland, actually. It's a tough state for such a place. We had an overall good experience with Rowdy at the local hospital, but my gut feeling was that this birth needed to be different. I wanted to feel close to my mom. I wanted to be like my mom. I wanted to be to my girl what my mom was to me. I found a birth center in Virginia, an hour away, that met all my 'needs,' desires, and more. I was swooning over the beautiful large rooms, lovely staff, helpful tools, and team of midwives. This was our place. I could feel it.

Summer was born a day early, like her Aunt Shannon. She was born at 4:00 in the morning. Her labor was much easier than her big brother's. It was important for me to be surrounded by "my people," particularly "my women" for this birth. And, amazingly, all four of my sisters and three of my closest friends were there. It might have been the only day in a multiple-week span that could have worked out as it did for their schedules. (And even then, Shannon was hours away at a soccer tournament and we had another set of our dear friends who were willing to fetch her so she could be with me. It takes a village!)

Mom always loved a good nap (or two!) so it was fitting that the only way my body really wanted to labor was when I was asleep (no joke). When I was finally at that white-knuckled, laid-out, every-fiber-of-your-body-in-use stage, I went to "the depths" once again. She came out in one big push and just like *that* it was over. I held her and I couldn't stop saying "I can't believe I did that. I can't believe I did that." Everyone around me was whimpering and gasping with a release of "wow!" tears. She was perfect. It was like the first time in history. No one could possibly have participated in something this big, this holy, this miraculous before! But, as it turns out, birth happens nearly every second of every day, all over the world. Women are laboring and delivering, laboring and delivering, bringing people across the metaphorical ocean to arrive at their destination: life.

Summer Jo Lee was named in honor of her grandmother she never knew, Suzanne Lee, as well as Caleb's little brother, Joel, who went to heaven when he was three years old. One of my favorite hymns refers to heaven as "fair Summerland." As the sun rose, our new family of four (Mom, Dad, big brother, and baby sister) were tucked into a queen bed in the birth room. Everyone fell asleep except for the adrenaline-oxytocin-filled Mom who had waited and waited to see this face. I just stared at her round, clementine cheeks and ran my finger along the bridge of her nose. As if she were a slow cold brew, and I didn't want to miss a single drop of her flavor. Heaven was near, the sunlight interrupted our cozy darkness, and we named her accordingly.

***

I suppose the grand connection and parallel between life and death is, well, obvious. Maybe I "missed" it because it's so commonly used in poetry or lyric or storyline. I had known of people who had died. Three of my four grandparents had died by the time my mom did. Schoolmates and classmates and Facebook friends and our church family had all lost precious lives, and I had gone to the funerals. But when losing Mom, I knew death for the first time, because I had really known her. I didn't just "know about" loss, instead loss was my friend. And in the exact same way, within months of the taking I got to personally know birth. I marvel still to this day, honestly many times a day, at how similar the two processes are. The tenacity of coming and going. The very first breath of air ever and the very last breath of air ever. The distinct smells only found at a birth or a death. The team of people coaching, comforting, supporting. The instant "loosing" when... it's over! Just like that, it's over! It's no small thing that Mom was moved at her core by birth, and then faced death with as much enduring, accepting, elegant, stable, fearsome strength as she had shown in bringing forth life.

It's a bit dicey to start to make a graph of "which is worse" when it comes to grief, but I know there are griefs worse than death. There are hardships more excruciating. I know there are "popular trials" and "unpopular trials" (the kind where you are rallied around and supported by a flood, and then the kind where you are very much left alone). I know there are deaths more traumatic. Ones where you don't get good-bye or closure or peace or relief or celebration. All you have is love being snatched away with no warning and I believe it's tremendously harder. It may sound strange to say, but I'm grateful for what I've been able to learn from what is hard about giving birth and what is good about dying. Because the goodness of birth and the hardness of death are self-evident, but getting to connect the dots and fill in the gaps has left me with such a profound picture of God and His heart.

The Message version of Isaiah 32:15 says "Yes, weep and grieve until the Spirit is poured down on us from above and the badlands desert grows crops, becoming fertile fields and forests. Justice will move into the desert. Right will build a home in the fertile field. And where there is Right, there will be Peace. And the promise of Right is: joyous lives and endless trust. My people will live in peaceful houses, in quiet gardens. You will enjoy a blessed life, planting well-watered fields and gardens."

Mom died to earth on January 22, 2014, but on the same moment she was born to heaven. Her Adoring Parent, eager Groom, and large family waited for her arrival. When she crossed from the outside of the pearly gates to the inside, Heaven was finally, completely, relieving-ly here. Not near! But HERE. And it was the best of everything, where not death, not demons, not cancer, not car accident, not anything in all creation could take away a moment of absolute joy. Where anything sad becomes untrue. And there she lives today in the City of Right, in her Home Country, in Summerland.

11. CONCLUSION

My first Mother's Day was a bit of a "triple whammy" in that it was indeed my first as a mother, it was the first since miscarrying (which had happened a week earlier), and the first since losing my mother. We were traveling, as we often are, and we found ourselves in Dallas, Texas.

Caleb planned a memorable day, starting with Sunday service at one of my favorite churches. Surrounded by strangers, and not knowing the name of a single soul in the room, I began to sing. We all did. The band led us in a song that was a new-hit at the time, and has grown very popular since — "Oceans" by Hillsong.

Ten days before, we had spent the night in a Los Angeles emergency room. Caleb saw our still baby on the ultrasound screen. Still babies on ultrasound screens are pretty awful sights. We had just wrapped up a sort of "getaway" trip and this was certainly not how we planned to conclude our refreshing time. I was getting phone calls and texts daily from my hurting brothers and sisters. They were a few months into navigating life without their I-Beam. At Mom's memorial service our dad directed his attention to us, the seven children. He said that if the Lord is the foundation of our home, then Mom was the giant, steel support running across the structure, holding the roof up. "We have lost our beam," he told us. "And no one person can do what she did. We all need to play our role, lift our hands, and hold up a part of ceiling. We need each other."

Families "coming together" and "rising up" when tragedy strikes is ideal, but not definite. We have referenced Dad's words often over the last two and half years as we have each grieved differently and at different times. There is no rulebook for playing the Game of Grief. I stood there that Sunday, my lightly-pooched belly empty, feeling such sadness for my brothers and sisters, whom I love nearly like children of my own. They, of course, are not my own and I am not their mother. But I can't help it. I am their sister. I love those kids; those kids who are growing up and making mistakes and accomplishing goals and figuring out this world and eating all the time and who are my favorite people to talk to. The hardest part of losing Mom, for me, has been watching them hurt. And… My baby died. I really wanted my baby.

The verses and choruses were sung with vigor, and the full auditorium had an inspiring energy. It was nice to sing. A balm to my sore heart. Then we collectively arrived at the bridge of the worship song. It goes as follows: "Let me walk upon the waters / Wherever You would call me. / <u>Take me deeper than my feet could ever wander</u> / And my faith will be made stronger / In the presence of my Savior."

And here's the crazy part: everyone was singing it. I did know the song beforehand, but as I thought about the words I actually closed my mouth and stopped. "Wait." I thought to myself, "Do… you realize what you are saying?" I looked around the room of casually but nicely dressed people. "You all are crazy!" I felt stunned to silence. I could not even speak the words "Take me deeper than my feet would ever wander." Nope. This is far enough! I'm…quite in over my head! And I would like very much to not be taken in any deeper than this! It's one thing to sing, for example, "You took me deeper than my feet would ever wander / And You made me stronger." But what was possessing everyone to ask for testing beyond what they would choose for themselves? Do you know what it's like to be in an ocean? And not be able to touch the ground anymore? And be stuck, unable to return to shore, as you're tossed in the waves? Well, you see, very few of us probably do know what that is like… because we don't wander that far.

It was being sung so easily, it seemed. So innocently. Maybe for some in the room it was just a soul-stirring idea that sounded fervent, especially with the slow and tugging instrumental. I know too much, however. I've seen too much. There are those who know what's at stake, who know what they are saying, and who sing anyway. "Wherever you would call me." They would go, and they wouldn't flinch. I saw my mom. I know. I watched her.

With no exaggeration, I can say with 100% (family-backed) honesty: Mom never complained about being sick, battling cancer, or dying. She didn't flinch. She was pulled far further than her feet would have ever wandered, or planned, and she meant it when she said, "I trust You." The presence of her Savior gave her courageous, wisdom, and peace.

It was as if she was living, enduring, singing, loving only for one pair of eyes. I remember countless times when she expressed to me, "I do not understand what God is doing, but I trust Him completely." She never doubted His constant, watchful eye upon her life. I witnessed the security with my own eyes. Mom was truly at rest in Who He Claimed To Be, and it was enough. With grace and humility she could admit to not being able to understand, but she knew He understood. She knew He was on the move, making all things new. She knew all would end well. "My soul will rest in Your embrace / I am Yours and You are mine."

As is hopefully and likely quite clear by now, being able to have my mother as "mine" was…everything. I remember when it dawned on me, as Caleb and I were dating, that the one he reminded me of was my mother. Not in a clingy or childish way, but rather he shared so many of the qualities that I respected and admired in her. She laid the groundwork for me, in what is my life today. Her reminders to "slow down" and "enjoy the moment" shaped my mind. Her attention to my heart showed me heaven. Her faith, oh her great faith, has given me roots. Her adventurous stories and cheer-leading gave me wings. No one has or will love me the way my mom loved me. I am so fortunate to have had her on my team, to have followed her as my leader, to have seen her face in the crowd.

I love you, Mama Bear.

Printed in Poland
by Amazon Fulfillment
Poland Sp. z o.o., Wrocław